The Heretic's Guide to Thelema

The Heretic's Guide to Thelema

Volume One:

New Aeon Magick
Thelema Without Tears

by
Gerald del Campo

Issued by order of
The Grand Triumvirate
of the Order of Thelemic Knights

Concrescent Press

Dedication
First Concrescent Press Edition

I dedicate his book to my loving wife, April, as well as Bonnie, Twayn, Liv, Jeff, Kim, Matthew and all other artists who labor at great personal cost to bring Beauty to a world drunk on misery. May your work continue to inspire others to do something better. We need you now more than ever before.

This book is dedicated to YOU.

Dedication & Thanks
2008 Edition

Dedicated to all the Children of Thelema, who are quickly becoming a formidable army and hold the seeds for a Thelemic Utopia in their hands. Learn from your parents, and plant them in fertile soil (The seeds, not the parents).

To Esperanza, for showing me that one can never be too old to be a dad and for reminding me of what is important. And to my soulmate April...who is still walks with me after all of this. For the life of me I have no idea what I might have done to deserve her. I love you.

And a very special thanks to the Secret Chiefs: Thanks...again. For everything.

This book is dedicated to you.

Contents

Other Thelemas
the publishers preface

It is a truism in the history of religions that they fracture on the death of their founder. Some even raise the question if a founder can even be a member of their own religion.

It is unsurprising therefore, that over one hundred years after the founding of Thelema by Aleister Crowley in 1904, we see a rich plurality of interpretations of the current. Some institutions attach deep importance to the founder and strive to follow his word so literally that they even forbid discussion of the scriptures. Some see it as a manifestation of the tantric wisdom of the Buddhadharma. Others, like the Chaos Magicians, interpret Thelemic antinomianism as a call to wild and wonderful experimentation. And these are hardly the only positions available in the extant range of practice.

In your hands is a work from a long-time practitioner of Thelema. It is a expression of his experience in a variety of forms of Thelema and a number of Thelemic institutions. As such it is uniquely his perspective, and for that reason it is being published. Not because it is right, or orthodox, or for any other reason but that is IS. The importance of this is that Thelema needs every form itself to be manifest in order for its full potential to be realized.

This presentation has a fairly martial character, yet has a strong sense of compassion. There is a certain sweetness in this first volume, as it was first written for the author's young children. Forthcoming will be work on the New Aeon English Qabalah and on the Ethics of Thelema.

Some will object, and thelemically, they are welcome to do so. But the Magi have always learned from Nature and so we must note that although Nature abhors a vacuum, She hates monocultures: She always and only destroys them. Variety and diversity only will strengthen the current of Thelema.

SUCCESS IS YOUR PROOF

A New Foreword to
the Heretic's Guide to Thelema

Greetings and Peace:

Do what thou wilt shall be the whole of the Law

Long ago, when I first wrote this book you are now reading, my aim was to bring Thelema out of the darkness that held it captive for so long. I wanted everyone to understand Thelema in their own terms, rather than being interpreted by the popular culture of the 90's, which appeared to cling on to Thelema only in protest of the Christianity that had been forced upon them by their parents, or the assumptions made about Thelema by the heavy metal songs written by artists who did not invest the time to get a good understanding of Crowley. I hope I am not misunderstood. I am a musician, and grew up with heavy metal. But those songs did little to portrait the factual life and times of Aleister Crowley, and were often based on writings by people who neither knew or understood him. All the musical movement did for Thelema was to create a following of angsty teenagers which viewed it as little more than a sort of mindless, disorganized Satanism. A sort of satanism that gave the real thing a bad name.

When the first edition of this work was published in 1994, it was one of the first books to deal with the subject of Thelema which did not exhaustively quote Crowley. It was the first book of its kind, and continues today largely due to fear of unkind criticism. In my mind, it is shameful that by and large, the loudest and most visible Thelemites would discourage any exploration into Thelema that did not regurgitate the material accepted and approved by the Crowleyan marketing machine. Anyone that has ever studied Thelema, already knows what Crowley thought of it, and how he interpreted it in his own time. It is time that each of us, individually, understood what it means to us. One of the greatest dangers that confronts Thelema, and by extension our own world, is that very few people will see it being relevant in their own time.

To address these issues, I wrote this little book. That was my contribution as an individual. The well established Thelemic collectives, however, approached these problems by trying to fit into the status quo and trying desperately to fit into our quickly decaying culture and putting on a professional corporate facade in an attempt to attract doctors, lawyers and other business types into their organizations. This meant securing semi-public venues so that meetings would take place in separate stand-alone buildings as opposed to having meetings and events in people's houses. This was a good move, in my opinion, if for no other reason that there is a certain liability incurred by inviting some stranger into ones home.

The problem no one could have foreseen is that to accomplish this task, it meant squeezing members for cash to pay for those semi-public venues. The blow-back[1] was that people were no longer valued or appreciated for being artists and bohemians. Instead, those that could help pay for those spaces became the new heroes, while the painter, musician, ritualist, and craftspersons that had advanced Thelema up to that point, became zeros. One can see the obvious error here. Religion is revolutionary. When its ambassadors stop using it to show an alternative world beyond the normal, it has lost its purpose. It becomes a cult by becoming one with the status quo.

In a work entitled "The Ethics of Thelema," I foresaw what would occur to American culture as a result of the mean-spirited Randian brand of libertarianism which would spread like a disease affecting every aspect of social-political life. It brought with it corporatism and fascism. The middle class blamed the poor for the recession and unemployment that would be created by the banks, the CEO's and the stockholders (which are implicit in the fiasco), until the middle class itself became the new "working poor."

Not surprisingly, in a rush to fit in and be all things to people with cash-flow, many Thelemic collectives have rushed to become EXACTLY like the society they wish so desperately to fit into.

In my mind, there is only one solution to deal with these problems head on. We must be more careful, this time, in choosing our heroes. I have said it again and again: Thelema holds the solutions to the problems we face today. The quoting of Liber AL or Nietzsche out of context isn't hard – in fact, in a way, those activities are mirrored in our overall culture today. The noble path, the way of the warrior is to tilt the scales of Justice to restore balance. Bring the artists, the musicians, craftspersons and Bohemians back to Thelema. What they

---

1   A military term used to describe the unintended reaction to ones action. In short, a kind of karma.

do, the social currency they bring and beauty that they create is what we need to take us forward to the days when Thelema will be a life-enhancing world force.

This little book has a surprising way of doing that. May it continue to do so long after I am gone.

Foreword to the 2008 Edition

Greetings and Peace:

Do what thou wilt shall be the whole of the Law

This edition you now hold in your hands is actually a compilation of three books. *New Aeon Magick: Thelema Without Tears*, which was published originally by Llewellyn in 1994, and then by Luxor Press in 2000, and *The New Aeon English Qabalah Revealed*, which was also published originally by Luxor Press and went through three printings in a period of two short years. The third book was first published by Immanion Press. It is called "Personal Thoughts on The Ethics of Thelema." So you might be wondering about the history behind the title of this compilation. I shall endeavor to explain it by going over some of the history of each book.

The first book, *New Aeon Magick*, was written upon my taking my third degree in the OTO, which is symbolic of death. This initiation left me thinking about what I would want my children (the oldest of whom was 6 at the time) to know about me if I were to pass on suddenly. I wondered what could be the best gift that I could leave them with, and decided that I would attempt to explain Thelema to them, so that when they were old enough to understand they would know why their father spent so much time with his head buried in those old dusty books, wearing a black dress, golden crowns, and strolling about with strange looking scepters while chanting strange words. Originally, the book was not to have any other audience than my kids. It was at the advice of my initiating officer that the decision was made to publish this book for the masses.

In the introduction I made sure to point out that this book had been written for my children, and that the information contained in those pages was composed to give people with no other exposure to Thelema a positive view of a philosophy and religion that I still consider today to hold the key to human evolution. In spite of the great effort I took to explain the intended audience for this book, *New Aeon Magick* received much unkind and unwarranted criticism by a small minority of intolerant Crowleyites who felt *New Aeon Magick* was not Crowleyesque enough to stimulate their supra-intellectual uber-minds. I had to wonder how the obvious fact that the book was written for my children could have escaped their intellectual prowess, but I simply accepted the criticism and moved on.

Concurrent with the negative opinion from the intolerant group mentioned above, *New Aeon Magick* enjoyed huge success from readers all over the world. My mailbox began to fill up with e-mail from readers (many of them Thelemites and OTO members) thankful of finally being able to grasp Thelema. I even received a few letters from readers who had adopted Thelema as a way of life, but dropped it after having joined a Thelemic group and found nothing worth emulating from the supposed Thelemic adherents and then came back to embracing it after reading this book.

From the time Luxor Press picked up the second printing until the day I left the OTO, *New Aeon Magick* was on the recommended reading list issued by the OTO's Public Information Officer. In 1997 it was adopted by the Pagan Student Alliance at the University of Texas. In 1996, the chapter on the Qabalah became recommended reading for a class on Jungian Psychology at the University of Cape Town, South Africa. *New Aeon Magick* contains something for everyone. Non-Thelemites have found the information on the Qabalah and comparative mythology to be an invaluable source of information they can use to make their way through their comparative religion studies.

New Aeon English Qabalah Revealed was published in 2001 in small quantities. I expected that this book would only be of interest to a small percentage of Thelemic occultists, since the method described within the book was bleeding edge technology. Most magicians like to stick to the classics and never seem to move on into uncharted territory. Imagine my surprise when this book went through its third printing.

This work received the same attention from the Thelemic community as *New Aeon Magick*. Up until the time that I left the OTO these books were proudly displayed on the US Grand Lodge web site, in a section dedicated to members who were also published authors. I believe that the bias against this book began as it became clear that the system exposed in this work originated with a note made by Charles Stansfeld Jones, (or Frater Achad as he was known in Crowley's magical order the A.'.A.'.) It did not begin or end with Crowley. In fact, the discoveries made while working this system often contradicted Crowley's comments on the text. People using the NAEQ on the Class A

material were finding that in spite of Crowley's attempt to force Thelema to fit his world view, much of it got through unhampered by his
personal prejudices in the form of a code or cipher.

If you understand the potential revenue for those who can control the Crowley legacy, you can begin to see why something like this
would not only be unwelcome but actually perceived as a threat or
competition to the Crowley marketing machine, not to mention the
aforementioned Crowleyites who cannot fathom a Thelema which ex-
tends beyond what Crowley might have known.

This, perhaps somewhat ironically, led to the thoughts which would
eventually become the material for the third work called "Personal
Thoughts on The Ethics of Thelema." It should be made clear from
the very beginning that work this is not an attempt for me to impose
my ethical ideas upon Thelema, but rather how I have formed my own
personal ethics based on my qabalistic discoveries, and magical work.
In short, Personal Thoughts on The Ethics of Thelema is how Thelema speaks to me, and I must warn you in advanced that once again
you will see that many of my ideas contradict the accepted "wisdom"
of Thelema being a philosophy for the uber-thug that goes around
stomping the weak and mocking the works of other religious paradigms without thought. If a Holy Book were to be taken literally, there
would be no point to studying magick or the Qabalah – no mystery…
no excitement of the chase, and not much of a holy book, either.
Thelema is not a religion for the intellectually lazy. To quote from
Personal Thoughts on The Ethics of Thelema:

> *All interpretative work must begin with a predetermined set of presump-
> tions: mine has always been that the Liber Al holds an lucid message,
> and that Law of Thelema contains within it the key to the survival of the
> human species; a noble warrior code; and a benevolent religion which is
> applicable to all who are willing to accept responsibility for their existence.*

Perhaps now you can see why *The Heretic's Guide To the Magick and
Ethics of Thelema* was chosen as the title of this work. Being a Thelemite
in my own time, by using my own mind, and basing my opinions on
my own work has made me a heretic in certain circles. I sincerely hope
that it makes a heretic out of you, because trust me, The Prophet
would have expected that from you, knowing full well that that nothing useful could come from adopting the prejudices of his own time,

and that if Thelema is ever going to evolve beyond the point where he brought it, then it needs to be just as relevant today as it was in his own time. Unfortunately, in my experience, freedom from organizational bias appears to be the only way to see things as they are.

Love is the law, love under will

Foreword to the 2000 Edition

Greetings and Peace:

Do what thou wilt shall be the whole of the Law

Much has occurred since *New Aeon Magick* first hit the bookstores in 1994. The response has been overwhelming. Never in my wildest dreams did I believe that this work was going to touch the heart of so many individuals. The fact that the response has been so positive simply points to a need in the Thelemic community, and within those of us who call ourselves "Thelemites."

I believe that individuals want Thelema to be in the hands of the masses, as Crowley clearly indicated. The Law is for all. It is not a tool to be used by a few for the purposes of intimidating, impressing, or otherwise controlling others. Everyone that accepts this Law has the responsibility to remove it from the darkness so that it may shine as a beacon for those to whom it is intended.

Should we strive to define Thelema for others? No, that is wisely forbidden to us. In an infinite universe, there are no absolutes; so far as Truth is concerned, there are only paradigms. Thelema will manifest itself within each of us in our own ways, according to our own psycho-spiritual development, and our ability to live our lives accordingly. Does this little book explain Thelema in its entirety? No. These are my ideas, or rather, were the ideas I wanted to convey to my three children when I wrote this book in 1993.

Think about this: What if everyone wrote a little book about how Thelema has manifested in his or her own life? There would be millions of books on the subject – each and every one as different as each of us. We cannot interpret Thelema for others, but we can be the living examples. Before you can live it, you must understand it in the Gnostic sense – you must know it so intimately that it defies the use of words. Read the writings of the Prophet. Perhaps we can be students by experience, teachers by example, as we ever expand our consciousness as Brothers and Sisters, Princes and Princesses raised under the roof of the same castle.

I have observed that in all things magical, there is a time for learning, followed by a many years of testing and proving, which ultimately leads to a period of reflection. It is almost like the cycle of birth, life, and death, itself. Except in a magician's case, the real life appears to begin with the period of reflection, the best time to write down experiences and share them with others of like mind.

But we must share information intelligently. How could we grow, otherwise? Since Thelema is differently manifested in each of us, how could we begin to understand what it is (or is not) without the input of other Thelemites? We could say that we should only concern ourselves with the way it illumines our own lives... but this is not acceptable for the philosopher, the Watcher. He wants to know it in its entirety.

The same can be said of magick. Oh, how many individuals labor under the assumption that only Crowley is entitled to write with any authority on the subject of magick, thereby overlooking the pearls thrown before them by the new magicians, philosophers, Thelemites.

You would be surprised at how many independent magicians come together in secrecy to discuss modern Qabalistic studies based on the logical hierarchy of numbers designated in our holy books. This system has been appropriately dubbed — NAEQ or —New Aeon English Qabalah, and it is worth a serious look by those of you who would like something new and refreshing. An Internet search for NAEQ will reveal much for interested parties.

Also know this: The minute you claim to be a Thelemite, you invoke a tremendous responsibility. You have just enrolled as an ambassador, and everyone will interpret what you say and do as something Thelemic. Big responsibility... and yet, in my mind, there is no greater privilege.

But what about the aspect of War that is so prevalent in the Thelemic Holy Books? You will have to interpret this in your own way. A person I am fortunate to call my Brother and friend once said:

> *"Someone read 'As Brothers fight ye!' and can you believe that some people took that to mean that we ought to fight amongst ourselves?"*

About the subject of war, I will just say this: There is no right in battle, for we all compromise some part of the thing that makes us human. Righteousness quickly flees the side of the idealist once the first human perishes in an effort to establish order. And despite this, war is a necessary part of the human experience. Doesn't make sense? That is the whole point. If we must fight, then let's fight for freedom, and let us fight like honor bound warrior-monks, not cowards that strike at the defeated and defenseless. Altruism is a necessary component in battle. It must, therefore, please Ra-Hoor-Khuit. Is Thelema a religion? Crowley appears to have thought so:

> *Do what thou wilt shall be the whole of the Law!*
>
> *Refuse this, and fall under the curse of destiny. Divide will against itself, the result is impotence and strife, strife-in-vain. The Law condemns no man. Accept the Law, and everything is lawful. Refuse the Law, you put yourself beyond its pale. It is the Law that Jesus Christ, or rather the Gnostic tradition of which the Christian-legend is a degradation, attempted to teach; but nearly every word he said was misinterpreted and garbled by his enemies, particularly by those who called themselves his disciples. In any case the Aeon was not ready for a Law of Freedom. Of all his followers' only St. Augustine appears to have got even a glimmer of what he meant.*
>
> *A further attempt to teach to his law was made through Sir Edward Kelly at the end of the sixteenth century. The bondage of orthodoxy prevented his words from being heard, or understood. In many other ways has the spirit of truth striven with man, and partial shadows of this truth have been the greatest allies of science and philosophy. Only now has success been attained. A perfect vehicle was found, in the message enshrined in a jeweled casket; that is to say, in a book with the injunction 'Change not as much as a style of a letter.' This book is reproduced in facsimile, in order that there shall be no possibility of corrupting it. Here, then, we have an absolutely fixed and definite standpoint for the foundation of an universal religion.*
>
> *We have the Key to the resolution of all human problems, both philosophical and practical. If we have seemed to labor at proof, our love must be the excuse for our infirmity; for we know well that which is written in the Book:*
>
> *'Success is your proof.'*
>
> *We ask no more than one witness; and we call upon Time to take an Oath, and testify to the Truth of our plea.*
>
> —*Equinox of The Gods*

Introduction

Do what thou wilt shall be the whole of the Law.

Magick may be described as a system of communication, a language used exclusively between the conscious (the logical mind) and the subconscious (the thinking mind). During dialogue, the magician's objective is to use his logical mind to convince the thinking mind to reveal a method by which to directly access the superconscious, the higher mind...the Holy Guardian Angel.

Every 2,000 years or so we enter into a new age. At this time, the subconscious changes, and so does the language to which it responds. Once this shift has occurred, the magician must make the necessary adjustments if he wants to keep the dialogue open. Should you fall into the rut called tradition (as many magicians do), you will no longer be able to affect those subtle forces that you are trying to stimulate, because you will no longer understand them.

In 1904, we entered such an age. The angel Aiwass[1] announced that Horus, the hawk-headed god, had taken his seat at the Throne of the Gods. The Aeon of the Child was upon us. As with most children, this one naturally had a rebellious attitude towards the old ways, and it insisted on creating new ways of doing things. The New Aeon brought with it a new law: "Do what thou wilt shall be the whole of the Law," and "Love is the law, love under will" (Crowley 2004). This unprecedented law demands the utmost discipline. It suggests that we each have a purpose, a will, and that we have a responsibility to follow that will, to live in harmony with the rest of the universe, and to be who we truly are.

By virtue of this law, not only are we freed from the bonds of ignorance the previous aeon brought, but it is emphasized that we protect our originality. The magical formula for the New Aeon must be structured in such a way that it can be distinguished from the old formulae, yet it must be capable of an overwhelming tolerance in order to allow great diversity.

The purpose of this book is to help you to discover the new language by which to communicate with your Self. This will help you to further understand the books already on your shelves, and most importantly, it will give you a foundation for creating your own unique

1 The discarnate being that dictated The Book of the Law.

methods. These methods will work better than anything learned from any book, because you will have created them for yourself. Although you will find ritual and instruction in this book, it is presented solely for the purpose of presenting the reader with some effective procedures. It is my hope that you will familiarize yourself with the mechanics involved in ceremonial magick, thereby becoming fit to design your own rituals.

Originally, I wrote this book for my three children, and for that reason you will find that I have written it in the second person; I hope this informality does not offend anyone. The purpose of this little work is not to show great literary skill, but rather to shed light on a difficult subject further obscured by authors looking for scholarly recognition. This limited volume does not contain all there is. No one could boast about having written such a book. You should simply view this as a primer.

The only thing that I ask is that you keep a diary. This will serve you by creating a book of spells and a reference that you can review to chart your progress along the Path. It will also serve those that come after you, by providing them with insight about an otherwise unknown approach. No matter how swiftly you have progressed, if you have left nothing to the next generation of magicians, then your contribution to the Great Work will have been limited to its evolutionary representation.

The magical path is a great road to travel; it has been frequented by many great names: Aleister Crowley, MacGregor Mathers, Dion Fortune, Helena Patrovna Blavatsky, Eliphas Levi, to name but a few. You will see their footprints along the way. It is my hope that this volume will encourage you to find your own path, so that you may open up a road not previously charted.

Love is the law, love under will

Gerald Del Campo
March 21, 1993
Ashland, Oregon

What Is Magick?

Religion is a daughter of Hope and Fear, explaining to Ignorance the nature of the Unknowable.

— Ambrose Bierce

Ask anybody what magick is, and the first answer you get will have to do with either the superstitious mumbling of the fanatical fundamentalist or the ridiculing rhetoric of the senseless skeptic. The skeptical fellow has one up on our fundamentalist friend in that he can still control some of the activity in his brain. There is hope for this one.

Aleister Crowley wrote such a thorough essay on this subject that I find myself incapable of adding anything that does not echo his definition. Read the introduction of his opus *Magick in Theory and Practice*.

Aleister Crowley defines <u>magick</u> as "the Science and Art of causing Change to occur in conformity with Will" (Crowley 1998).

Ambrose Bierce defines <u>magic</u> as "An art of converting superstition into coin" (Bierce 2002).

Notice the difference in the spelling.

To distinguish illusionary magic from real magick, Crowley chose to use the Elizabethan variation of the word, distinguishing it from slight of hand magic by adding the letter k at the end. This changes the numerical value of the word and, as such, should be studied.

You must keep in mind that magick demands repetitious study. It is foolish to assume you have understood something unless you have read it several times and have been able to achieve the same results every time you use it. Do your experiments as though you were a scientist in a laboratory. *Keep a diary!*

Magick is the method by which all things (be it conscious or not) exist and live their lives. Magick will allow you to recognize who and what you are so that you may realize your full potential; however, it will not transform you into something you are incapable of being.

So much beauty and mystery is found in the surviving literature of those who practiced the Craft that many artists are instinctively drawn to magick by verse and song. Ceremonial magick is the great struggle of evolution given physical expression in a mystical dance; it is the essence of what we have been and what we are now, and it is the attempt to assist Nature, Our Great Mother, in our *becoming*, via self-discovery and via an active role in our own further development.

To help you understand how magick works, I must say a few things about the mind. Not only does the brain store memory, it is also capable of behaving as a receiver. It registers memory, and then executes the appropriate response. Thought and information are maintained within our cells. Our DNA carries within it not only genetic information, but specific experiences, thoughts, and patterns of personality from our parents. This is often what a person experiences in past life episodes. The brain picks up genetic information once our cells release energy (memory). The brain does all this in its effort to answer those haunting questions: Who am I? Where do I come from? Where am I going?

Each cell is a separate, living, conscious life form, just as we are. The problem is that we are not, as a rule, consciously capable of releasing the data within the cells.

For the most part, we are created and shaped according to other peoples' fancies. This shaping starts very early in childhood when our parents (being ignorant of their own wills) impose certain restrictions and limitations on us that may not have anything to do with our True Selves. As a result people live their lives to please those around them instead of recognizing who they truly are. The longer we are forced to do this, and the deeper we hide ourselves, the harder it is for us to find who we truly are.

There are three series of manuscripts which, together, have become the source of knowledge for the modern day magician. They are:

- The books of Solomon (*The Key of Solomon the King* and *The Lesser Key of Solomon*)
- The writings of John Dee
- and *The Book of the Sacred Magic of Abramelin the Mage.*

The books of Solomon are believed to have been written between 100 and 400 AD. They are based on the myths found in the Old Testament, the Talmud, and the Koran revolving around Solomon the King, the author of Proverbs, Ecclesiastes, the Song of Songs, and Wisdom.

With the assistance of demons subdued by a ring given to him by the angel Raphael, Solomon built a temple dedicated to the evocation, prosecution, classification, and identification of malignant spirits. This manuscript included information as to what names were used to call the spirits and constrain them, as well as an elaborate hierarchy based on their power and abilities. Solomon forced demon after demon to concede its name, power, and the name of the angel who could be called to control it. This work is seen as the greatest contribution to ceremonial magick by those who practice it, as it is a complete genealogical tree and a source for Persian, Greek, Jewish, and Christian mythology.

The second series is a compilation of elusive writings received from 1582 to 1587, during several crystal gazing sessions by two Elizabethan magicians named John Dee and Edward Kelly. Dr. Dee anticipated that one could better communicate with the angels of God if one could speak in their tongue. He hired Edward Kelly, a medium, to communicate with various angels who would eventually divulge their language: Enochian. This strange speech was believed to be the language that Adam used to communicate with angels before the Great Fall.

With the help of several angels, Dee and Kelly were able to compose five elemental tablets describing a hierarchy of specialized angels who could be summoned to the service of the magician.

The names written on these tablets were so powerful that they were given to Kelly in reverse, for it was believed that the angels could be accidentally invoked by concentrating on the strange characters composing their names. Even today, experienced magicians heed this warning and dabblers are discouraged from the use of Enochian magick for their own safety.

The third manuscript, *The Book of the Sacred Magick of Abramelin the Mage*, was written by Abraham the Jew and presented to his son Lamech in 1458. It is very likely that Abra-Melin was to Abraham what Aiwass was to Crowley—a discarnate being who communicated specific principles to its human counterpart.

This manuscript was found at the Bibliotheque de l'Arsenal in Paris and was translated from its Hebrew form to French during the 17th or 18th century. Later, MacGregor Mathers translated the French copy into English.

Perhaps the most significant contribution made by this book is that, while it is emphasized that one become familiar with Qabalistic principles, the author strongly recommends that the student use and consecrate his *own* language by using it in these rites. It is universal in its message that any student, whether Jewish, Christian, or Pagan command and exercise authority over the demons mentioned in the book by using the Names of Power associated with his faith.

The manuscript was divided into three books. The first book contains personal advice from Abraham to his son and an account of how he came by this knowledge. The second book is perhaps the most important from a seeker's point of view; it is a complete treatise on the methods used to access magical powers. The third book deals with the implementation and management of this capacity.

Like the books of Solomon and the Enochian works of Dee and Kelly, the book of Abra-Melin the Mage is outdated in that it subscribes to the doctrine that one must isolate oneself from society in order to accomplish the Great Work. In spite of this apparent Old Aeon dogma, the importance of this book cannot be underestimated, for it was through the practices laid out in this manuscript that Aleister Crowley achieved Knowledge and Conversation with his Holy Guardian Angel.

An aside: There appears to be a tradition of burning one's works at the time of one's death. Both Solomon and Dee are rumored to have burned their memoirs. If this is true, then one would think that what we possess of these great men and women is very little in comparison with what must have perished by fire. For one reason or another, on April 10, 1586, Dee burned all of his works. However, according to the chronicles left behind, on April 30, while strolling through a garden in the castle of Trebona, Dee *found* the books he had deliberately burned on the 10th.

Among other things, magick is an ancient form of what is currently referred to as *psychoanalysis*. It is often used as a means to free the real Self from the self created by others. The magician takes a hidden, and sometimes hideous, part of his consciousness (in Goetic work, the evocation of demons) and externalizes it to better deal with it. Through magick, he makes the necessary adjustments to become a healthier and better balanced individual.

Magick is the way we can obtain consciousness of the activity and infinite wisdom within us all. And by doing so, magick helps us to see ourselves as we truly are so that we may plot our course accordingly.

As soon as you recognize the deity within, you will find that you have been in control the whole time, but have not responded well due to your lack of understanding. It is like driving with a blindfold. The strength of your will is measured by your ability to respond (rather than react) to your environment. When you embrace life, and when you can willingly experience it as it is, then you will have embraced with Our Lady of the Stars.

The Qabalah

*Nothing is a secret key of this law. Sixty-one the Jews call it; I call it
eight, Eighty, four hundred & eighteen.*

— Liber AL I:46

It is hard to pinpoint the exact date of the creation or the origin of
the Qabalah; however, the earliest Qabalistic manuscript in our cus-
tody is called the *Sepher Yetzirah*, otherwise known as the *Book of Forma-
tion*. This text is thought to have been compiled around 120 AD from
much older manuscripts, by a man called Rabbi Akiba.

The most crucial book to the study of the Qabalah is called the *Zohar*. While this manuscript was not penned until the late 13th century
by Moses de Leon, it is the most significant treatise connecting Gnosticism with other ancient mystical systems.

The Qabalah is unique to Hebraic thought. Traditionally, it is
thought that the teachings were brought out of Egypt by the Israelites. During the Babylonian captivity, the Israelites borrowed the Chal-
deans' use of a system of numerology called *gematria*.

It is worth mentioning here that the Biblical hero Moses was raised
as an Egyptian and was taught the mysteries of that race of people.
Later, his own clan versed him in Hebrew mysticism. Perhaps it was
the combination of those systems that enabled him to become such a
powerful figure in history.

According to ancient Hebraic tradition, God Himself first disclosed
the Qabalah to the angels. When man was taken out of Eden, God allowed the archangel Ratziel (the archangel of Wisdom) to divulge its
secrets to the human race as a means for them to find their way back
to the Paradise they had lost.

The Qabalah is unique to Hebraic thought and, as you will notice,
it uses a lot of Hebraic language and symbolism. However, we will not
limit its use by dwelling too much on the dogmatic aspects of this ancient system.

The reason for ignoring dogma is quite simple: the Hebraic faith
has used this model for quite some time, and the impressions from
the thousands who have meditated on the symbols are there for us to
access. During the centuries, especially during the medieval era, the
Qabalah was widely dispersed throughout Europe.

Magicians and their apprentices of every school of thought have
meditated upon its symbols, adding to it the archetypes unique to

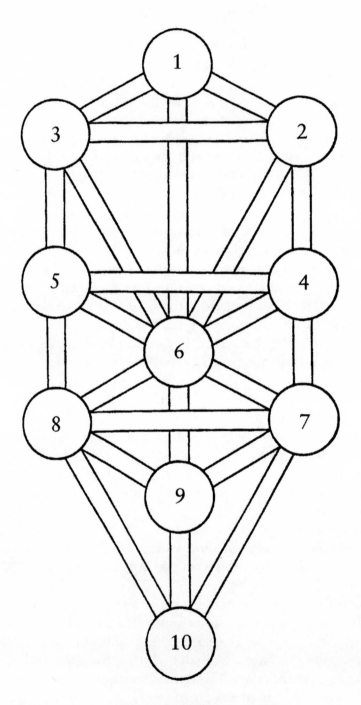

The Qabalistic Tree of Life

their systems. For this reason, the Qabalah is richer in metaphysical wisdom than ever.

The Qabalistic icon of the *Tree of Life* is frequently mentioned in the Old Testament. This tree contains ten fruits called the *sephiroth* (emanations), which have been referred to as 'the ten faces of God,' and since humans were created in the image of God, the Tree of Life is a metaphor for the body of man (see illustration).

These ten emanations are symbols that illustrate the vigor and power of the creative energy inherent in the first sphere, Kether, the Crown, moving as swiftly as a lightning flash, changing with every step through the ten varying phases, coming to completion at the tenth sphere of Malkuth, the Kingdom. The map of the tree attempts to describe the creation of the Universe, and those who have studied science will have to admit that, as primitive as it may be, it serves as a basic symbol illustrating the big bang theory. These spheres are connected by 22 *paths*. The paths correspond to the Tarot's Major Arcana.

In a way, the sephiroth attempt to describe certain traits of the Most High, or the Universe...or both. They are here listed in order from the Beginning, where the whole of Creation is concentrated to a minuscule point, to the End:

1.   Kether: Crown.
2.   Chokmah: Wisdom
3.   Binah: Understanding
4.   Chesed: Mercy
5.   Geburah: Power
6.   Tiphareth: Beauty
7.   Netzach: Victory
8.   Hod: Splendor
9.   Yesod: Foundation
10. Malkuth: Kingdom

The union of Kether, Chokmah, and Binah illustrates the manifestation of the Universe. This merger composes the *Supernal Triad*, which is often referred to as God ('Elohim') in Genesis. The remaining seven sephiroth represent the seven days of creation in the legend of Genesis.

The Hebrew Qabalah is used liberally throughout four of the five Biblical books attributed to Moses. The reason for its very limited use in Moses' book of Deuteronomy is unknown.

In magick, the Qabalah is used as a filing system with which one can synthesize any phenomenon whatsoever, no matter how abstract, and break it down into terms that can be understood by the logical mind.

This system enables us to tap into the forces and currents symbolized by the particular symbol we are working with. The magician looks up the correspondences to the sephirah and uses the information to invoke that particular current.

This use of Qabalistic correspondences is a science created on the premise that there is an existing inherent relationship between planets, metals, stones, animals, flora, colors, and aromas. The implements, tools, incense, and colors that the magician uses will thus be in some way connected with the sephirah which best conveys his Will. This will be explained in more detail later.

Since the alchemists perceived illness to be caused by a planetary imbalance, they also used this system to find cures for the ill. The cures were created by balancing the energies from the planet responsible for the disease, and then using the herbs and potions attributed to the sephirah representing the opposite planet on the Tree of Life, thus finding balance.

While the Qabalah is not essential to magick, it will help you to understand associated phenomena. It is a system of correspondences that enables us to encounter the macrocosm by close scrutiny of the microcosm: As above, so below.

The Qabalah used in magick bears little resemblance to the Kabbalah practiced by early Jews. It enabled medieval practitioners to have some conscious control over how the unconscious mind stored and retrieved data, by providing a perfect filing system. This was a major breakthrough and a giant step forward for those individuals who dared to explore the darkest recesses of the human mind. Magicians from all schools embraced this technology, and added to it symbols and attributions unique to their systems.

The destruction of the obstacles that keep the conscious and unconscious from working together in harmony has been a preoccupation throughout the ages, as it is now. The important thing to remember about the Qabalah is that the way it communicates to the Higher Self will greatly depend on how intimate one is with the information attributed to the sephiroth.

Regardless of the methods employed, one must first find a philosophy that resonates with the one's inner nature as a magician. For the Rosicrucian, it is Mystical Christianity; to the Thelemite, it is the message of Aiwass.

The first approach is to familiarize yourself with the methodology of the Qabalah until you understand why the ideas and symbols placed upon the tree fit and network the way they do. By its use and study, you will begin to see patterns, and will realize that the placement of a particular symbol or archetype is validated and supported by the surrounding sephiroth. It is like trying to assemble a puzzle containing the essence of the whole universe, using the pieces already in place to verify whether the next piece you place will be in harmony with the rest of the puzzle. You simply use the symbols already in place, whether Roman, Greek, Hindu, etc. to see how they apply to the philosophy and archetypes you have embraced.

In other words, after studying and understanding the system as laid out by our predecessors, the student applies the symbols most harmonious to his own inner nature. If these are properly arranged, they will be faster and more powerful when employed. However, the student must be careful not to alter the infrastructure of the system; it works like no other, and the wrong manipulation could alter its effectiveness and hamper the ability to communicate to the mind. These operations appeal to magicians because magicians have inquisitive natures. They are not happy with the knowledge that something works, but must find out why. This application must be approached using the methods of science.

Magicians must learn to view tradition in its proper context. The function of tradition in magick is to ensure the continuance of viable, workable systems – not their dogma. Because the Qabalah has been so enriched by our forerunners, our minds are capable of evolving much faster than ever before. It is ridiculous to assume that we would evolve beyond the achievements (and shortcomings) of our predecessors unless we added our own, personal, unique symbolism to the Tree of Life.

To quote the psychoanalyst Carl Jung:

We can never legitimately cut loose from our archetypal foundations unless we are prepared to pay the price of a neurosis, any more than we can rid ourselves from our body and its organs without committing suicide. If we cannot deny the archetypes or otherwise neutralize them, we are confronted, at every new stage in the differentiation of consciousness to which civilization attains, with the task of finding a new interpretation appropriate to this stage, in order to connect the life of the past that still exists in us with the life of the present, which threatens to slip away (Jung 1976).

I believe that the Qabalistic system is perfect. It works. The beauty of the Tree of Life is that familiarity with one sephirah will yield clues pertaining to the qualities of its neighboring sephiroth and the paths. Therefore, the student should not strive to replace these symbols, but new, compatible symbols should be added. What is a symbol? It is a representation or model capable of depicting something unknown.

Those that follow us will equally benefit from our experiences, until they too find themselves having to attribute their own unique correspondences to this glyph. This is evolution at work, and hopefully, those with the right stuff will create new myths that will propel the species into a harmonious future.

I am not implying that the works of Fortune, Mathers, or Crowley are worthless; it is virtually impossible to speak in Qabalistic terms without referring to their correspondences. Their work and efforts have given us a treasure house of knowledge regarding the mechanics of the system *and* hidden truths of the philosophies they embraced; they have provided a universal language that all Qabalists can use to communicate abstract ideas. How else could master magicians instruct their apprentices without divulging their own justifications and methods? We stand on the shoulders of giants.

One should work with the available literature to familiarize oneself with the process. Crowley's *Liber 777*, for example, is an excellent instructional manual which illustrates the methods and reasons that Crowley attributed specific gods to the ideas and symbols of the sephiroth, and one should learn this method of association. This not only involves mastery over the Qabalistic system, but also the study of the world's mythologies and the use of those most harmonious with the character of the magician.

Also, keep in mind that there is nothing wrong with combining mythologies. In the past, many cultures have either openly borrowed or taken by force the customs, traditions, and habits from neighboring societies and attributed to them different names. They have simply taken the archetypal form symbolized by a particular god, and have renamed it the name of a deity with a similar nature.

The Greeks borrowed from the Egyptians, the Romans from the Greeks, and so on. Often, the names were not even changed – much less their attributions. Some are so similar that it overwhelms the mind to keep them separate. A glance into the study of historical mythology will make one aware of the similarity between some of the Greek and Roman Deities.

If you are interested in developing your own system of correspondences, you will have to study the mythologies of the world. There are many untouched mythologies for magicians with a pioneering spirit, for example Phoenician, Celtic, Teutonic, Slavonic, Persian, Indian, Chinese, Japanese, and African deities (for those who prefer Voudon Magick). There is even a tireless group of individuals working a system of English Qabalah, which we will address in book two of this compilation.

Every religion maintains a sparkle of universal truth in its symbology; one may borrow from as many as is practical to the end desired. The modern magician should feel free, as the Romans and Greeks have, to unite as many systems as he feels is needed to personalize his own Qabalah. The only rule is to make sure the deity is in its proper place and that it is polarized by its counterparts so that the surrounding placements do not negate the placement of one deity. Errors will be easily recognized when the system is tested and the discrepancies are not capable of being reconciled.

Many magicians understand the need for evolution of magick. Much new work is already underway, and we will eventually start to see new authors publishing the Qabalistic significance of Santerian and Voudon archetypes. Work has begun in the area of Rune Magick, and the system of English Qabalah has already been mentioned. As a result of these new additions, those familiar with Qabalistic principles will finally be able to exploit these systems, and I think that we can predict an increase of interest as magicians learn to understand these ideas in Qabalistic terms.

If you are a purist, study the myth that works best for you, and attribute its deities to their proper places on the Tree of Life. Keep notes on *why* you placed them there – the flaws and imperfections will become visible through your practices. Record trials and errors in your magical diary, until your system becomes a perfect extension of who you are.

A magician must maintain distaste for dogma and the stagnation it creates in psycho/spiritual evolution. This attitude is as crucial in magick as skepticism. There are few students who dare to step beyond the normally accepted methods of attribution because every previous method has been exploited and published, only to be taken as gospel truth. Many of the best examples of outdated traditions can be found in the Bible.

Like all Holy Books, the objective of the Bible was to incorporate the traditions associated with a particular society and combine it with a supernatural purpose in order to chart and ensure the survival of the community it represented. It is a survival book for a race of people, imparting a knowledge and systematic lifestyle specifically designed to preserve and protect the evolutionary struggle of a culture that was trying to rise above the norm.

The other factor most Holy Books have in common is the us–versus-them syndrome. This is where the Deity dictating the book divulges the information that the proponents of the religion are better than the surrounding folk, and that God only favors them. Usually some instruction is given as to how to deal with the heathens, and violence is justified in the name of God. In short, people who opposed a particular belief, philosophy, or religion also opposed the way of life it represented.

There have been people who did not possess warrior-like skills or the organizational skills to conquer or prevent from being conquered. Their Holy Books do not tolerate violence of any sort – even in self-defense. This is also a survival formula... albeit, not a very effective one.

So what happens after technology surpasses the Holy Book? What shall we do once our capacity to rise above and beyond the ideas represented by its morality reveals that the teachings are no longer valid and are therefore untrue? Should we close our eyes to common sense or forsake the laws of nature for the benefit of tradition? Must we sacrifice or retard our own development as a species? Or should we apply what we have learned to a changing world?

The attitudes toward human sexuality in the Old *and* New Testaments illustrate how useless (and sometimes destructive) dogma and tradition can be to human development. Morality laws that attempt to regulate our erotic natures are no longer applicable. Biblically, any sexual act that failed to produce fruit (workers) threatened the survival of that race. Similar objections are found throughout *The Torah* with regard to eating certain types of food. In short, any behavior that did not contribute to the benefit the whole community was prohibited. These policies ensured the perpetuation and survival of the community.

Now, the world has reached its population capacity. It is no more advantageous to criticize sexual practices that are nonconductive to human reproduction than it is to prohibit the consumption of pork; and yet, because of tradition, the Christian churches still prohibit the use of birth control and sex education.

Like all living things, religion must be capable of adapting to new circumstances as humankind's knowledge increases. The evolution of the human race depends on mythologies that are malleable and pragmatic. Dogma is an intoxicating, but often fatal cocktail composed mainly of a paradigm with a twist of tyranny and a splash of fanaticism.

All holy books contain Truths. Truth is *always* faithful; it is unchanging and omnipresent. It is only the *understanding* of Truth that changes as we evolve. I do not believe abandoning the older Holy Books is the answer. We must reinterpret them using what we know of the Universe, Nature, and the human race today. Truth is ever becoming, even as we are.

New religious systems, and their principles, must adamantly reject old, expired thoughts that did not stand the test of time. They must also be flexible enough to embrace any original principles and truths that continue to push us toward perfection. I perceive Thelema as such as system.

Many teachers (some called Adepts) discourage individuality, stifling their students' creativity until they become part of the larger herd mentality of the magical community. This is a great injustice to the Art of Magick, as some of the greatest potential discoveries are nipped in the bud before they can yield fruit.

The purpose of the following treatise is to encourage exploration and to display the process without reaching *any* conclusion; although these ideas, principles, symbols, and archetypes are functional as they stand, they are here implied solely as guidelines.

The mysteries embodied in religion and philosophy are encrypted to keep what is sacred safely out of reach of foreigners and heathens with contradicting ideas. I have found the Qabalah to be an encryption and decryption *key*, which will, when used properly, yield many wonders, including a peek into race consciousness of the creators of the philosophy you are exploring. I cannot over-emphasize the tremendous power of the Qabalah when individualized by the use of personal archetypes.

The magician's greatest assets are his imagination, conviction, dedication, endurance, commitment, and a healthy dose of skepticism. Magicians will often express or use intangible concepts by assigning them to mythological ideas or Gods in order to achieve a desired result. These ideas serve to communicate to the specific part of the psyche the archetypes represent. That the magician *believes them* is *imperative* to the success of the operation.

There must be no doubt in the magician's mind that he believes in these ideas. If the magician 'stops and asks why' the operation is doomed. If he spends too much time thinking about whether the desired effect will manifest, *Lust of Result* will set in. He must not only *believe* in the intangibles he has created, but must *know* beyond a shadow of a doubt that the desired result will occur.

And herein lies a dangerous curb in our path. Voluntary mental irregularity is relatively harmless to well balanced individuals who have practiced Magick for many years. These mental states are self-induced, and due to mental and physical preparation of the mind and body, one is ready for the journey. Most importantly, well prepared magicians never lose track of the fact that what they believe is a *paradigm.* One must never forget that one is accepting intangibles as truths for the convenience of getting a desired effect.

A magician whose intellect will not let go long enough to allow him to create a necessary scenario for his magick is in little danger of falling over the edge, but his magick will simply not work. It takes something more powerful than reason.

A magician who achieves successful results only does so because his myth has become *a living thing.* He has breathed life into it by virtue of belief, conviction, and Work. Once this is accomplished, the magician has found the foundation on which to base his life's work.

I will present the curious reader with a system of correspondences illustrating the mechanics of the Qabalah, while simultaneously providing a practical manual for magicians who intend on using these correspondences for the purpose of performing practical magick, all in a condensed format that will serve readers *and* arm the practical magician with a reference he can use in ritual.

Simply turn to the pages intended for the sephirah that best encompasses the end desired, then use the correspondences to inundate the Temple (and the psyche) with the appropriate incense, plants, stones, weapons, squares, etc.

You will find a Recommended Reading list on page 203.

A Word about Balance

In magical circles, much has been said about Hod and Netzach – Intellect and Emotion. This is probably due to the fact that the first obvious polarity people encounter on the Path is that of Reason and Intuition. Plenty of good advice is given as to how to coexist with people of one or the other inclination. It has become a subject worthy of controversy, and for good reason. Hod could be seen as Law, and Netzach as Love – Science and Art.

That familiar quote from *Liber Al vel Legis,* "Let one not know well the other" (Crowley 2004), has become the favorite form of justification for those too lazy to find Balance. It helps them perpetuate the myth that these opposites cannot or should not be reconciled. I have heard it mentioned that practical magick is, by nature, a Hod activity. This may be true in the Qabalistic sense, when specific functions are assigned to the sephirah for the purpose of scrutiny, but to say that magick can work without emotional juice is not only false, but purposely misleading.

Crowley's definition of Magick is: "The Science and Art of causing change to occur in conformity with Will" (Crowley 1998). Science alludes to Hod, and Art to Netzach. Meditation on the Art Tarot card will reveal this (and many other mysteries), as both principles are therein embodied. While magick has much to offer those adept in mathematics, geometry, Qabalah, astrology, etc., it has just as much to offer those who move instinctively and are sensitive to the energies and images around them – those adept at Tarot, I-Ching, and other methods of divination. They rely not so much on the Hod activity we call 'intellectual knowledge,' but trust in the inner voice of the Beloved to guide them through life, shape the clay, guide the brush, and provide the lyrical content for words of wisdom.

Music serves us as a perfect model, as it is a child resulting from the unity of Science and Art. Music is defined and created by following certain mathematical principles. Without knowledge of mathematics, music becomes random noise, incapable of stirring the emotions. This is a Hod function. Without the sublime understanding of the function of sound and its effects on the brain and nervous system, music becomes two-dimensional, boring, incapable of holding our attention – a poor form of expressing love, joy, sadness, anger, etc.

The emotional nature of music is Netzach's contribution. Ignore the mathematical aspects of Hod and you get noise. Ignore the intuitional expression of Netzach and your music will lack depth and emotional content. Balance is the basis of the Work. Those of us who are intellectual by nature should aspire to use this Hod function to stimulate the emotional aspects of Netzach. Failing to do so would make us cold, calculated and callused, incapable of feeling the subtle energies stimulated by our magick. We'd be nothing more than thinking machines, unable to hear The Voice within because it does not fit our logical mold. One could be lost in Its simplicity.

On the other hand, those of us who are of an emotional nature should use this Netzach purpose and employ it to stir the discriminating genius within us all. Should we fail to accomplish this task, we run the risk of becoming little more than foolish idiots, gullible to the point of abuse and superstitious to the level of schizophrenia. We would not recognize The Voice of The Beloved or the intricacy of Its language, thereby falling prey to the demons of deceit.

I would suggest that what is needed is the understanding of when to employ unshakable scrutiny and skepticism, the wisdom to know when to toss all of that aside, and the strength to do them both.

It is far healthier to be intellectually and emotionally balanced *as individuals*, than to justify a lack of balance by attaching to groups that over-emphasize the point of balance within the group as a whole. If you remember nothing else you have read in these pages, always keep in mind that Thelemic magick is a system that holds the highest regard for the individual. Dion Fortune made a brilliant observation describing the need for balance:

> *"The purely female woman and purely male man proved to be oversexed as judged by civilized standards, and can only find an appropriate place in primitive societies, where fertility is the primary demand that society makes upon its women, and hunting and fishing are the constant occupation of the men."*

Remember: specialization is for insects.

Those of you practicing Thelemic magick in groups, remember that, from a magical point of view, the amount and quality of the energy you generate as a group will be much more powerful and much saner if *each* of your members is encouraged towards intellectual and emotional balance, rather than trying to adjust to the lack of individual balance by enrolling equal numbers of members who may be lacking one or the other of these qualities. Thelema is primarily concerned with the growth of the individual, not the masses.

I hope this book will provide the necessary foundation to begin your magical studies, and that whatever path you chose will lead you to the accomplishment of your True Will – The Great Work.

KETHER

Meaning:	The Crown
God Name:	Eheieh
Image:	Ancient Bearded King (in profile)
Titles:	Existence of Existence Concealed of Concealed Ancients of Ancients Primordial Point The Point Within The Circle Most High Macroprosopos LVX Occulta LVX Interna
Archangel:	Metatron
Order of Angels:	Chaioth ha Qadesh, Holy Living Creatures.
Spiritual Experience:	Union with God
Virtue:	Completion of The Great Work
Vice:	None
Human Chakra:	The Cranium
Magical Weapons:	The Crown The Point The Swastika
Incense and/or Oil:	Ambergris
Precious Stone:	The Diamond
Plants:	Almond Flower
Tarot Cards:	The Four Aces

KETHER

Kether is the only sephirah that manifests from an unknowable source: the Veils of Negative Existence. Kether is, however, understood through an experience the Hindu Adepts refer to as *Samadhi.*

It is pure being, timeless, totally devoid of form because it exists above Binah, which is Time, and Chokmah, which is Form. It is one degree removed from non-existence. (The other sephiroth are further removed from non-existence as we get closer to Malkuth.) Because it is without form, it exceeds the laws of manifestation – it is without reaction. It does not conform to any of the criteria we use to define existence. It is presence. It is the cause of manifestation, but it is not the manifested.

Existence is measured by its opposite. Kether has no opposite that we can measure it against, and therefore, one can only know its functions according to its connection to the other sephiroth.

The other sephiroth are only extensions of Kether. It is easy to understand this whole premise if we view Kether as the source of Light. As the Light moves away from The Source, the vibrations of that Light decrease until, upon reaching Malkuth, the Light is so dense that it appears to be solid.

The Crown was attributed to Kether to illustrate the fact that it is beyond consciousness – the Crown is worn *above* the head. That is why the Mundane Chakra is the Cranium – the uppermost part of the human head.

The Adepts have said that Kether is of our cosmos, but not in it. This indicates that those who attain to its influence exist in a state beyond duality, which occurs in everyday life, and are able to rise above the senses and experience the perfection of the Universal condition.

It is the source of all magical energy, which specializes as it moves through the lower sephiroth. Dion Fortune has warned that anyone who misuses this energy by using it against universal or natural law will pay accordingly by losing the corresponding energy from their own being (Fortune 2000).

Kether has always been associated with the terrible gods that consume their own children because the universe emanates from it, and is eventually reabsorbed by it.

CHOKMAH

Meaning:	Wisdom
God Name:	Jehovah
Image:	A Bearded Male Figure
Titles:	Abba Supernal Father YHVH Yod
Archangel:	Ratziel
Order of Angels:	Auphanim, Wheels
Spiritual Experience:	The Vision of God Face to Face
Virtue:	Devotion
Vice:	None
Human Chakra:	Left side of the face
Magical Weapons:	The Lingam The Phallus The Yod of YHVH Inner Robe of Glory The Standing Stone The Tower The Uplifted Rod of Power The Straight Line
Incense and/or Oil:	Musk
Precious Stone:	The Star Ruby
Plants:	Amaranth Flower Mistletoe
Tarot Cards: **Wands (Fire):** **Cups (Water):** **Swords (Air):** **Disks (Earth):**	The Four Twos Dominion Love Peace Change

CHOKMAH

Kether's symbol is the Point, and since a point in motion would look like a straight line, the Straight Line was chosen as an appropriate symbol to illustrate Chokmah's relation to Kether.

Because Chokmah is the giver of life, we find it on the right side of the Tree of Life, called *The Pillar of Mercy*. The image of the bearded male signifies virility. It is the vessel for Kether's influence, and symbolizes the beginning of life and its transition towards matter. It is the archetypal Father – active, positive force.

The *Sepher Yetzirah* states that Chokmah is pure being and not a thing in itself (Kaplan 1997). After reading about Kether one may think that this is a contradiction. This further connects it to Kether. Chokmah is Kether at the precise moment of being and not-being – Chaos.

Kether is energy, and Chokmah is the conduit for the passing energy, the influx of cosmic fuel, and as we will see, Binah is a reservoir which stores and catalyzes that energy.

BINAH

Meaning:	Understanding
God Name:	YHVH Elohim
Image:	The Crone; A Mature Woman
Titles:	Ama: Dark Sterile Mother Aima: Bright Fertile Mother Khorsia: The Throne Marah: The Great Sea
Archangel:	Taphkiel
Order of Angels:	Aralim, Thrones.
Spiritual Experience:	Vision of Sorrow
Virtue:	Silence
Vice:	Covetousness Greed Avarice
Human Chakra:	The Right Side of The Face
Magical Weapons:	The Yoni The Keteis The Chalice The Outer Robe of Concealment
Incenses and/or Oils:	Myrrh or Civet
Precious Stones:	The Star Sapphire The Pearl
Plants:	The Cypress The Opium Poppy The Lotus The Lily
Alchemical Metal:	Lead
Tarot Cards: Wands (Fire): Cups (Water): Daggers (Air): Disks (Earth):	The Four Threes Virtue Abundance Sorrow Works

3 – SATURN

4	9	2
3	5	7
8	1	6

BINAH

Binah is The Primordial Mother, and therefore represents the creative forces of the universe. She is The Cosmic Womb, The Universal Vagina, Babalon. Binah is Negative – form. Chokmah is Positive – energy. Binah is the fertile soil, and Chokmah is the seed. The title of those that attain to Binah is Magister Templi; they are often referred to as Nemo (no-man) and it is their duty to tend the garden.[1]

She (Binah) introduces energy to solid matter, which subjects it to death; hence the name, "The Terrible Mother." Because disembodied spirits are immortal, and only through incarnation does life experience death, Buddhists and Christians have unjustly sneered at Binah.

Because the planet Saturn has been attributed here, the uninitiated have given her the titles Set, Shaitan, and Satan. And because all creations are subjected to the influence of time, Christianity in its vulgar form (as it exists today) views woman as the source of all evil, the enemy of the omnipotent spirit of man (Chokmah). Form is the discipline of energy, and it is for this reason that she is placed at the head of The Pillar of Severity.

Death is a byproduct of sex, and it is implicit in birth; the Angel of Death is with us from the very beginnings of our physical lives. Astrologers cringe at the thought of Saturn making a comeback into their charts.

In the Qabalah, all sephiroth are equally holy, and Binah is perceived as the function that has allowed everything below it to participate in this thing we call "life." Binah is a necessity for evolution. She is the essence of Kether taking form. She is the beginning of all matter that is not realized until Malkuth. This is further illustrated by the fact that The Universe Tarot card connects Binah (Saturn) to Malkuth. The *Sepher Yetzirah* also tells us that Malkuth is the Daughter of Binah (Kaplan 1997).

Binah represents faith – faith as described by a knowing which is beyond words, ineffable. A feeling not yet intellectualized, as in unexplained emotional reactions.

---

1 The Cry of the 13th Aethyr, Which is Called ZIM: "And he saith: No man hath beheld the face of my Father. Therefore he that hath beheld it is called NEMO. And know thou that every man that is called NEMO hath a garden that he tendeth. And every garden that is and flourisheth hath been prepared from the desert by NEMO, watered with the waters that were called death." .

She is the Virgin Mary of the Christian faiths. She maintains her virginity because she is not concerned with the life of her creation. She remains pure by virtue of the fact that she performs her function according to her nature; like all the other sephiroth, she does her True Will. In this context, a prostitute who is doing her Will is much purer than a chaste woman whose hidden nature is unbridled passion. Impurity is a loss of control, a straying from one's True Path that can only be corrected by self-knowledge. Impurity comes from the phenomenon of attempting to override one's inner nature. Celibacy and sex are recognized tools to achieve God Consciousness.

In her opus, *The Mystical Qabalah,* Dion Fortune states: "Frigidity and impotence are imperfections just as is uncontrollable lust, which destroys itself as well as its object. Reproduction is a sacred process, and the ancients referred to it with reverence" (Fortune 2000). Hence, the creative process of Binah is not evil, but necessary to the evolution of the spirit, which is symbolized by the rest of the Tree.

CHESED

Meaning:	Mercy
God Name:	El
Image:	A King Upon A Throne
Titles:	Gedulah: Love Majesty
Archangel:	Tzadkiel
Order of Angels:	Chasmalim, Brilliant Ones.
Spiritual Experience:	Vision Of Love
Virtue:	Obedience
Vices:	Bigotry Hypocrisy Tyranny
Human Chakra:	The Left Arm
Magical Weapons:	The Pyramid Tetrahedron Wand, Scepter & Crook
Incense and/or Oil:	Cedarwood
Precious Stones:	Lapis Lazuli Amethyst Sapphire
Plants:	The Olive The Four Leaf Clover The Opium Poppy
Alchemical Metal:	Tin
Tarot Cards: Wands (Fire): Cups (Water): Swords (Air): Disks (Earth):	The Four Fours Completion Luxury Truce Power

4 - JUPITER

4	14	15	1
9	7	6	12
5	11	10	8
16	2	3	13

CHESED

Chesed contains all the Holy Powers, and from it emanates all Spiritual Virtues with the most exalted essences.
– Sepher Yetzirah

The Tarot trump The Hierophant best describes Chesed's functions. It represents control in both secular and religious matters; therefore, it is often invoked to achieve favorable rulings in court. It receives direct influence from Binah, Understanding, and it is this influence that makes Chesed so benevolent.

Christian mystics place Jehovah upon this sephirah because it encompasses the attributions given to their God: The Vision of Love, Obedience, etc. We can also see how the vices manifest upon that belief system when they are interpreted crudely: Bigotry, Hypocrisy, and Tyranny. Dion Fortune speculated that if a magician should reach Tiphareth without attaining or progressing to Chesed, he would find Jesus the Personal Savior in the sphere of the Sun, and demand that others do the same. The magician is in danger of interpreting Tiphareth *as* Kether, rather than a manifestation *of* Kether.

Chesed is generous, like the King who has so much of everything he is willing and eager to give to those in need. Since Chesed is the first sephirah below the Supernals, it represents the formulation of divine ideas into concrete terms, hence its attribution to The Hierophant.

Because of this closeness to the Supernals, magicians who have attained to the sphere of Chesed are capable of glimpses into the big picture. Due to this awareness, we are told that they have escaped the bounds of physical reality, the bonds of birth, life and death, and are capable of choosing not to reincarnate. This is misleading because of the implication that one has achieved perfection, but one's placement below the Supernals demands a certain amount of imperfection, a human quality one transcends when rising beyond the Abyss and attaining pure consciousness.

Magicians attaining to Chesed can interpret the archetypal symbols emanated from the Supernals as mathematicians interpret algebraic models. *Obedience* here refers to the ability to recognize the obvious – to attain to the higher principles defined by the Supernals, one must push aside the Ego. In this case, the wishful thinking of what things are or what one imagines them to be, in order to receive or interpret the archetypal images and ideas for what they truly are. It is a sacrifice of a freedom not conducive to the attainment ones desires.

GEBURAH

Meaning:	Severity
God Name:	Elohim Gebur
Image:	A Warrior on a Chariot
Titles:	Din: Justice Pachad: Fear
Archangel:	Khamael
Order of Angels:	Seraphim, Fiery Serpents
Spiritual Experience:	Vision of Power or Strength
Virtues:	Energy Courage
Vices:	Cruelty Destruction
Human Chakra:	The Right Arm
Magical Weapons:	The Pentagon The Five-Petaled Rose The Sword The Spear The Scourge & Chain
Incense and/or Oil:	Tobacco
Precious Stone:	The Ruby
Plants:	The Oak Hickory The Stinging Nettle
Alchemical Metal:	Iron
Tarot Cards: In Wands (Fire): In Cups (Water): In Swords (Air): In Disks (Earth):	The Four Fives Strife Disappointment Defeat Worry

5 – MARS

11	24	7	20	3
4	12	25	8	16
17	5	13	21	9
10	18	1	14	22
23	6	19	2	15

GEBURAH

Since this is the most misunderstood of all the sephiroth, it is the most important.

— Dion Fortune, *The Mystical Qabalah*

Traditionally, Geburah has been a subject of controversy because it represents the Ego, the sex drive, and the destruction of the useless. Because Christianity failed to recognize the necessity of these functions, they were dubbed evil, and so was the sephirah that represented them. At best, the Christian church perceived it as the sphere of sacrifice motivated by fear, which can only be interpreted as an act of cowardice in the Aeon of Horus. As a result of this misunderstanding, the malicious Greek God of War, Ares, was assigned to Geburah. (See the section on the Greek Gods in Chapter 4)

Consider how astrologers interpret Mars in a chart — it is almost always considered malicious, and they do much to correct this malignancy when it occurs in their diagrams. Observing Geburah's influence in the four elements through its Tarot Card attributions does little for its defense.

We must avoid the perception of evil when referring to any sephirah, and this is especially true of Geburah. Most sephiroth in their purest essences are, by themselves, imbalances. This is particularly notable when the sephirah in question exists anywhere else than the Middle Pillar. No energy can exist without its opposite extreme, and never forget that any attempt to ignore the influence of any imbalance will only magnify it.

Consider this:

1. The manipulation of energy in a manner unnatural to its design is evil.
2. The magi realizes that the removal or absence of any energy or idea out of his immediate universe creates a vacuum which, out of necessity, must be filled.
3. The magician uses these paradigms to consciously create vacuums. By removing unnecessary things, desirable energies and influences can be invoked in their place. One thing is *sacrificed* for another.

The three points above illustrate both the necessity and the application of Geburah in magical work. Geburah is The House of The Will.

So how do you explore the potentialities of Geburah without injury? Like all sephiroth, you must study it by comparing it to the surrounding energies. The first logical place to look would be Chesed, its opposite. Looking at the attributions therein, you would prepare accordingly to enjoy the experience of Geburah without hardship. (See the notes on Balance on page 39.) Geburah is the driving force behind all action. It is the warrior that demands from us the respect mandated by The Holy Guardian Angel. It is through its influence that we are driven towards reverent acts of worship, such as Bhakti yoga (devotional yoga), which will inevitably lead us to Knowledge and Conversation. Hence, we see Mars' connection to Venus.

Geburah represents the Kundalini. Absolute vitality, it is the energy residing at the base of the spine waiting to spring forth. Without it, love in its sexual form would be unachievable. It is said to be transformed to the True Ego by virtue of orgasm; it is during those brief moments of ecstasy (the little death) that we are capable of piercing the veil of illusion.

Christianity has inaccurately explained destructive energy to be bad and creative force to be good. Geburah is concerned with the release of energy through the catabolic process of physics, and from this we can reaffirm its connection to the Kundalini.

It is easy to perceive Geburah as the martial arts teacher whose job it is to keep its students well balanced. When students stray from their natural paths, the teacher brings them back in the most expedient manner; when the phenomena is unpleasant, we may perceive it as 'evil.' Anyone who has ever taken martial arts can attest to this metaphor.

Geburah is known as *The Radical Intelligence* because it is the discriminatory part of the psyche. Physically speaking, it is better to submit to the scalpel than to perish by a malignancy. Geburah is a pragmatic sphere; it represents the destruction of the worthless to make room for the priceless, and here we see a resemblance to Kali.

When misunderstood, it can be painful, but if one is able to see beyond the struggle and suffering, the helpful aspects are visible. Existence is always moving and shifting. Geburah represents this movement.

It is the power of the steam engine, whereby wood is sacrificed and transformed into heat, which changes water into steam, which in turn drives the pistons. In this way, Geburah teaches us that energy can be transmuted but never destroyed. This alludes to the concept of Immortality.

Sacrifice is here intended to mean a necessary act willingly performed so that its energy can be redirected and used for achieving more desirable objectives. For the offering to be effective, it must be more than just a convenient act of self-denial – it must consciously be carried out as an act of devotion.

Tiphareth

Meaning:	Beauty
God Name:	YHVH Aloah Va Da'ath
Images:	A Majestic King A Child A Sacrificed God
Titles:	Malek; The King Adam; The Son
Archangel:	Raphael
Order of Angels:	Malachim, Kings
Spiritual Experience:	Vision of Harmony
Virtues:	Devotion to The Great Work Knowledge & Conversation with The H.G.A.
Vice:	Pride (more accurately, Arrogance)
Human Chakra:	The Heart
Magical Weapons:	The Cube The Rosy Cross
Incense and/or Oil:	Olibanum, Frankincense
Precious Stone:	The Topaz
Plants:	The Oak The Acorn Acacia The Laurel The Grape Vine
Alchemical Metal:	Gold
Tarot Cards: **Wands (Fire):** **Cups (Water):** **Swords (Air):** **Disks (Earth):**	The Four Sixes Victory Pleasure Science Success

6 - Sol

6	32	3	34	35	1
7	11	27	28	8	30
24	14	16	15	23	19
13	20	22	21	17	18
25	29	10	9	26	12
36	5	33	4	2	31

Tiphareth

Tiphareth is the point of balance on the Tree of Life; everything above it can be perceived as energy, and everything below it, as tangible. It is the link connecting God with Man, and as a result, Christian Mystics have placed Jesus on this sphere – as are all sacrificial gods. It is the sphere where one achieves Knowledge and Conversation with The Holy Guardian Angel; it represents the sixth sense and the Higher Self. It is the reflection of the flame that burns within the heart of man. It is the part of a human which is consistent and unchanging. It comes as no surprise that many magicians have confused this sephirah with Kether.

Tiphareth is like a lens that projects the Light from the Supernals unto the physical planes – as above, so below. However, we must not lose track of the fact that a projection of a thing is an illusion, and not the thing itself (Fortune 2000).

The image of a Child is a handy reminder that Tiphareth is referred to as 'The Plane of Incarnation.' Here we also find all sacrificed gods, because giving up perpetual existence to experience physical reality is considered a sacrifice – temporary mortality. God reveals itself (or appears to be) as flesh and blood and resides with the community, all the while imparting knowledge. But again, one must never confuse the vision of the thing with the thing itself.

In Christianity, it is said that one can only know the Father through the Son, and this nicely alludes to Fortune's statement about the lens, but it also reaffirms that Kether is the Father, and Tiphareth the Son. The magician's task is to become the Son (Tiphareth), so that he may know the Father (Kether). Magicians do this by bringing the rest of the sephiroth into perfect balance within themselves. The magician becomes the redeemer by trying to unite the kingdom (Malkuth) with heaven (Kether).

To avoid psychosis, all visions should be interpreted while on the plane of Tiphareth. It is the safest place to reside, because it has absorbed all of the attributions represented by the surrounding sephiroth. It maintains all of the discriminatory faculties of Geburah, tempered by the benevolence of Chesed, and the emotional nature of Netzach, tempered by the intellectual awareness of Hod. Armed with these tools, the magician is in little danger of perceiving the visions as physical, and will perceive them as symbols, as they should be.

Knowledge and Conversation rarely leads to visions or voices; the experience is full consciousness and awareness. The experience is not psychic, which is the trademark of Yesod; the absence of sensory images is a hint that the magician is in the level of higher consciousness belonging to Tiphareth.

Knowledge (of Knowledge and Conversation) refers here to the biblical sense – sexual intimacy. Every experience is brief, and the ecstasy soon fades, but there is that which remains. The mineral attributed to Tiphareth is Gold – incorruptible and imperishable.

NETZACH

Meaning:	Victory
God Name:	YHVH Tzabaoth
Image:	A Strong, Naked Amazonian Woman
Titles:	Firmness Occult Intelligence
Archangel:	Haniel
Order of Angels:	Elohim, Gods
Spiritual Experience:	The Vision of Beauty Triumphant
Virtue:	Unselfishness
Vices:	Unchastity Lust
Human Chakras:	Hips, Legs
Magical Weapons:	The Lamp The Girdle The Rose The Seven Veils
Incenses and/or Oils:	Red Sandalwood Rose Benzoin
Precious Stone:	The Emerald
Plants:	The Rose The Vine
Alchemical Metal:	Copper
Tarot Cards: **Wands (Fire):** **Cups (Water):** **Swords (Air):** **Disks (Earth):**	The Four Sevens Valour Debauch Futility Failure

7 – VENUS

22	47	16	41	10	35	4
5	23	48	17	42	11	29
30	6	24	49	18	36	12
13	21	7	25	43	19	37
38	14	32	1	26	44	30
21	39	8	33	2	27	45
46	15	40	9	34	3	28

Netzach

Magicians often pay very little attention to the Venusian sphere. Its vulgar interpretation has led many Qabalists to perceive Netzach as the 'cushie feelie' sephirah. Its magical image is that of a strong, naked Amazonian woman, which indicates immediately that the underlying current is definitely female, but certainly not passive.

Netzach rules the emotions, which empower the elemental forces by allowing them entry into consciousness. Were it not for Netzach, these elemental forces would remain in the unconscious realm of Yesod, where they would be free to raise havoc with our psyches. By emotions, I mean involuntary reactions brought about by active groups of symbols or ideas that reside in the unconscious (Yesod).

It is through Netzach that elemental administrators receive their life. It must be understood that the elemental influences receive their force from Netzach via the magician's emotional triggers.

Without Netzach, the magician can only create forms, but is not able to breathe life into them, and this alone should emphasize its function and importance.

This is the sphere of sympathetic magick and the intuitive residence. Magicians who resonate favorably with the sphere of Venus are instinctively drawn to the works of Bhakti yoga – devotional forms of worship.

The part of the psyche that corresponds to Netzach responds to sound, fragrance, and color. During a Netzach working, the Temple will be filled with incense smoke and the sound of rhythmic drumming, oftentimes ending with a frenzy of dance and laughter.

It seems appropriate that all goddesses of love are attributed to this sphere, since the Kundalini force *Ida* corresponds to it. The implements relate to the goddesses – The Lamp to Psyche, The Girdle to Aphrodite, The Rose to Venus, and The Seven Veils to Ishtar.

In the Babylonian myths, Ishtar lost her lover Tammuz when he descended into the underworld. She sought to reunite with him and demanded entrance into the lower world, which had seven portals, and was forced to surrender one veil at each portal. The veils and gates represent the seven primary chakras. The rose, which is connected to Netzach, is the Western equivalent of the Eastern lotus. A symbol for love, the rose verifies the notion that the Kundalini is stimulated by the act of lovemaking.

It is impossible to perform magick without the Netzach function, which corresponds to the instincts, because the skepticism embodied by its polarizing sephirah (Hod) will cancel out all magical imagery before it is even consciously realized. By way of the intellect, the magician creates talismans, but it is Netzach that breathes life into them.

Hod

Meaning:	Glory (Honor)
God Name:	Elohim Tzabaoth
Image:	A Hermaphrodite
Title:	Perfect Intelligence
Archangel:	Michael
Order of Angels:	Beni Elohim, Sons of God.
Spiritual Experience:	Vision Of Splendor
Virtue:	Truthfulness
Vices:	Falsehood Dishonesty
Human Chakra:	Legs
Magical Weapons:	The Names Versicles & Apron
Incense and/or Oil:	Storax
Precious Stones:	The Opal
Plants:	Moly
Alchemical Metal:	Mercury
Tarot Cards: Wands (Fire): Cups (Water): Swords (Air): Disks (Earth):	The Four Eights Swiftness Indolence Interference Prudence

8 – Mercury

8	58	59	5	4	62	63	1
49	15	14	52	53	11	10	56
41	23	22	44	45	19	18	48
32	34	35	29	28	38	39	25
40	26	27	37	36	30	31	33
17	47	46	20	21	43	42	24
9	55	54	12	13	51	50	16
64	2	3	61	60	6	7	57

HOD

The magical weapons connected with Hod allude well to its function. One can only name something once it has been given form, and Hod gives elemental forces form.

The Apron is usually worn over the genitals, which are portrayed by Yesod, the astral sphere that represents unconscious imagery – something unknown. The Apron signifies that these unconscious images are transcended as they are given Force by Netzach and Form by Hod; they have been released and utilized. From a practical point of view, Hod creates the talismans, while Netzach animates them.

Dion Fortune made a brilliant comment concerning the Apron and its relation to Hod. She stated that the Apron is the regalia of the Mason, a maker of forms, and therefore justified quite nicely its placement as a weapon or tool of this sphere (Fortune 2000).

The connection to form should not confuse the reader. Binah is the giver of form. Hod is the reflection of Binah after it has been filtered through Chesed. Hod is the intellectual manifestation of a spiritual idea represented by Binah. This is another way of saying that Binah's domain is within the Nashama,[1] while Hod exists in the Ruach.[2]

You may be wondering why Binah is filtered by Chesed and not Tiphareth. The mystery lies in what Binah, Chesed, and Hod have in common: the element of Water. The same is true of Chokmah, Geburah, and Netzach because all three share the element of Fire. The Middle Pillar consists entirely of sephiroth corresponding with the element of Air, and these principles apply here as well. Do not allow this to confuse you. (See the diagram of Elemental Attributions.)

One of the many attributions to the sphere of Mercury alludes to the intellect – the capacity to reason, the seat of logic. It is interesting to note that it also represents the Kundalini energy known as *Pingala*.

The vices of falsehood and dishonesty probably allude to the God of Thieves, Mercury, who received a bad reputation in Greek mythology for having stolen the heifers of Apollo. (See Chapter 4.)

The Archangel Michael was probably placed here because he is the slayer of the serpent, and illustrates the superiority of the intellect over illusion.

Because the intellect is greatly embellished by this sephirah, it has

1 The Highest Aspirations of The Soul.
2 The Mind, or The Ego.

become a trap for many potential magicians. Many of them will become armchair magicians, satisfied with the never ending task of impressing their fellows with their mental prowess. This is mental masturbation, and does not lead to Knowledge and Conversation of the Holy Guardian Angel. The magician must be constantly aware of this danger, and strive as best as he can to continue moving forward. (See a Word about Balance on page 39 .)

YESOD

Meaning:	Foundation
God Name:	Shaddai El Chai: Almighty Living God
Image:	A Beautiful Naked Man
Titles:	The Treasure House Of Images Levanah
Archangel:	Gabriel
Order of Angels:	Kerubim, The Strong
Spiritual Experiences:	The Discovery of The True Will The Vision of the Universal Machine
Virtue:	Independence
Vice:	Idleness
Human Chakra:	The Reproductive Organs
Magical Weapons:	The Perfumes The Sandals
Incense and/or Oil:	Jasmine
Precious Stone:	Quartz
Plants:	Damiana Ginseng Yohimba Mandrake (all aphrodisiacs)
Alchemical Metal:	Silver
Tarot Cards: Wands (Fire): Cups (Water): Swords (Air): Disks (Earth):	The Four Nines Strength Happiness Cruelty Gain

YESOD

Yesod is the unconscious, the house of the instincts, The Treasure House of Images. Instincts are an unintentional push towards certain activities, and are therefore of particular importance to the magician, as the ultimate task is freedom from impulsive behavior. The unconscious can be defined as the sum of all objects and routines that are not conscious or related to the Ego in any sensible manner.

In the individual, Yesod represents the sexual drive and all other survival reflexes. It is also the home of the racial consciousness, or Jung's collective unconscious, which he discovered "contains the whole spiritual heritage of mankind's evolution, born anew in the brain structure of every individual" (Jung 1970). He, too, saw the potential of tapping into ancient potencies for the betterment of the individual, and described two methods to study the collective unconscious – mythology and analysis. The magician uses both techniques.

It may appear to the Ego that it controls the faculties over the personality, but Yesod provides the data, or more appropriately, the images by which the Ego reacts to specific stimuli. Dion Fortune rightly perceived Yesod to be a filter that funnels in all ideas and experiences collected by the sephiroth above it, reconciling opposites "without diminution or separation" (Fortune 2000). So strong is the influence of this sephirah on our behavior and perceptions that the ancients assigned words of strength whenever possible; even the magical image associated with Yesod depicts great power. Instincts, impulses, dreams, visions and psychic awareness are attributed to this sphere, as it is considered to be the astral plane.

9 – LUNA

37	78	29	70	21	62	13	54	5
6	38	79	30	71	22	63	14	46
47	7	39	80	31	72	23	55	15
16	48	8	40	81	32	64	24	56
57	17	49	9	41	73	33	65	25
26	58	18	50	1	42	17	34	66
67	27	59	10	51	2	43	75	35
36	68	19	60	11	52	3	44	76
77	28	69	20	61	12	53	4	45

Makuth

Meaning:	Kingdom
God Names:	Adoni Malekh Adoni Ha Aretz
Image:	A Beautiful Young Woman, Throned & Crowned
Titles:	The Inferior Mother Malkah: The Queen Kallah: The Bride The Gate Gate of Death Gate of Tears Gate of The Garden Of Eden Gate of The Shadow Of Death Gate of Justice Gate of The Daughter of The Mighty Ones
Archangel:	Sandalphon
Order of Angels:	Ashim, Souls of Fire
Spiritual Experience:	Vision of the Holy Guardian Angel
Virtue:	Discrimination
Vices:	Avarice Inertia
Human Chakras:	The Feet The Anus
Magical Weapons:	The Equal Armed Cross The Double Cubed Altar The Magick Circle The Triangle
Incense and/or Oil:	Dittany of Crete
Precious Stones:	Rock Crystal
Plants:	The Willow Wheat The Lilly The Pomegranate
Tarot Cards: Wands (Fire): Cups (Water): Swords (Air): Disks (Earth):	The Four Tens Oppression Satiety Ruin Wealth

Makuth

Malkuth is so consequential in so many planes that it would take many tomes to list every possible correspondence. Like all other sephiroth, it is ever becoming, and no one could ever assume to know everything there is to comprehend about any of them. Even if such a book could be written and published, it would be a considerable detriment to magicians, because knowledge can only be understood when discovered and experienced by the individual.

Because it is the physical representation of the magician in his physical form, Malkuth is equated with the body. It is the sphere of the elements, so it is also connected with the planet Earth. It represents the fruition or completion of any magical action, so it is connected to the manifestation of spiritual ideas into concrete forms. It is connected to childbirth, eating, breathing, living, and dying.

Gematria

Divide, add, multiply, and understand.

— *Liber AL* I:25

Although Gematria is congruent to the Qabalah, I think it should be treated as a separate issue, to better illustrate the practical aspects of this wonderful system. The theory here is that any words that enumerate to the same value have something in common. Perfect examples of this are found all throughout the Holy Scriptures in statements such as, "God is Love," or "Love is Unity." The idea behind gematria is that words can be replaced with other words of the same numerical value, thus revealing certain hidden mysteries. One is not limited to the Hebrew language; this method of Qabalistic analysis can be used on just about any holy book, as long as one becomes familiar with the numerical value of the language it was written in.

The ancient Jews did not use numerical symbols. Instead, they attributed numerical values to their already existing sacred alphabet. Unfortunately, this system is perceived by the vulgar only as another form of numerology, thereby disregarding the complexity, beauty, and brilliance of such profound thought.

The importance of the use of gematria cannot be overstressed, especially when attempting to unravel the mysteries of the Bible. The authority of Biblical interpreters who are unfamiliar with Qabalistic principles, and yet claim to have fully disclosed its teachings, is questionable. Here is why: The Pentateuch was written in Hebrew, and most of the works show the use of the Qabalah.

The English interpretation (or any other but Hebrew, for that matter) lacks the numerical symbolism of the words written therein. They are lost in the translation; therefore, the inner meaning of the Scriptures cannot be understood by anyone not possessing knowledge of the system.

One would make a great error in assuming that this form of analysis does not apply to the New Testament because it was written in Greek. There is also Greek gematria, and there is evidence that it was used in the New Testament. Here's an example from the book of Revelation (6:2); it deals with the Four Horseman of the Apocalypse. "And I saw, and behold a white horse; and he sat on him had a bow; and a crown was given unto him: and he went forth conquering, and to conquer."

This particular passage deals with three crucial clues: the color white, the bow, and the crown. The color white is the color of Light, representing purity and cleanliness. The bow is a symbol of Sagittarius the Archer, or one whose arrows are pointed at spiritual targets. It represents the longing to attain to spiritual heights. "Crown" is *Kether* in Hebrew, the first, white sephirah on the Tree of Life.

So, as you can see, the Scriptures take on a completely different meaning when you understand the methods with which they were written.

It is not necessary to become fluent in Hebrew, Latin, or Greek, but it wouldn't hurt to be at least familiar with the Qabalistic correspondences of the letters of these ancient languages.

I thought Malkuth might be a practical place to illustrate some of the uses for Qabalah and Gematria.

The numerical value of Malkuth is 496. It is the same enumeration as the Hebrew, mythical, serpent-like creature called Leviathan. From this, we see its connection to Da'ath.

Its Mystical Number is 55. The same number as the Hebrew words meaning:

- Robbery, Thief, and Pillage – suggesting both the lust for *and lack of* substance and physical belongings.
- A Footstool, or To Walk – We walk with our feet upon the Earth.
- The Bride – A title of Malkuth.
- To Swell, or Heave – Implying its connection to manifestation, or childbirth.
- Ornament – Referring to the fact that Malkuth is the only solid sephirah on The Tree.

We have been told that Malkuth is the sphere of the elements. We can therefore assume that the Hebrew letters associated with the elemental attributions on the pentagram will yield further clues. So we add them up as follows:

Fire: Yod = 10
Water: Heh = 5
Air: Vav = 6
Earth: Heh = 5
Spirit: Shin = 300
                  —— 326

So we look up the correspondences to the number 326, and we yield the name Jeheshua – Jesus – and this confirms the probability that a god can walk among us.

Even if we assume that the element of Spirit must reside in some higher, more perfected plane, we can yield fruits from an analysis of the Hebrew letters in Tetagrammaton, and the numerical value of this analysis will reinforce the conclusion that Malkuth represents the concrete ideas represented by the whole Tree, just as the number 55 has. (1+2+3+4+5+6+7+8+9+10 = 55)

Fire:	Yod	=	10
Water:	Heh	=	5
Air:	Vav	=	6
Earth:	Heh	=	5
			—— 26

The Hebrew word for "seeing" or "looking at" enumerates to 26, and this validates our claim of Malkuth being the only solid sephirah. The number 26 also points us to the four directions, which are so important to magical operations, by alluding to the astrological signs that represent them:

East:	Air:	Aquarius:	The eleventh sign:	11
South:	Fire:	Leo:	The fifth sign:	5
West:	Water:	Scorpio:	The eighth sign:	8
North:	Earth:	Taurus:	The Second sign:	2
				—— 26

What else does the number 26 tell us? It alludes to The Middle Pillar:

First sephirah:	Kether:	1
Sixth sephirah:	Tiphareth:	6
Ninth sephirah:	Yesod:	9
Tenth sephirah:	Malkuth:	10
		—— 26

Malkuth is the physical body. In the efforts to provide their adherents with a philosophy that accurately describes the indescribable, many philosophers have been confused by the intense desire of the human spirit to unite with The Source. This bewilderment has resulted in the complete disregard for the human body, because they have failed to see that there is no separation between the Physical and the Spiritual. The human body is viewed as a prison to the omnipotent spirit, yet, how omnipotent is a spirit when it can be confined by something as frail as a human body?

As I have stated elsewhere, Kether is one step removed from existence. Malkuth is existence, and everything between them signifies stages of becoming. Kether is in Malkuth, and Malkuth in Kether.

I have interpreted physical existence as The Beloved's spiritual adventure, fueled by the desire to experience life in material terms. Until such a time that the physical body has been spent, we should *live* in such a way as to gain as much experience as humanly possible. Experience is Knowledge. Existence is pure joy. Sorrow is Knowledge without Understanding.

If you look at the Tree of Life, you will notice that each sephirah has a Hebraic name, and each path has a Hebrew letter assigned to it. To reap the fruit from this Tree, you will have to labor to master its language. There are only a few correspondences to commit to memory, and I have listed them for you elsewhere in this book to facilitate reference.

To conserve space, I have only demonstrated here a single form of analysis, but there are many others you will soon develop as you use this system.

We now continue with the association of various deities to the sephiroth.

The Gods

A brief look into mythology is all that is necessary to understand the considerations and justifications for the Qabalistic placement of the gods. The following information should begin to reveal the method for creating and expanding, and ultimately, personalizing your own Qabalah.

What follows is a summary, and the reader should be aware that *777 and Other Qabalistic Writings of Aleister Crowley* often shows the same god on more than one sephiroth. I hope that this does not confuse anyone. It wasn't done as a blind for the uninitiated, but to give the magician more options. Several deities can be invoked to assist in any particular task, and by studying the mythological functions of the deities attributed to the sephirah in question, the student can chose an archetypal image that comes closest to the end desired.

Take Zeus, for example. In Liber 777, Crowley placed him in Kether and Yesod (Crowley 1986). This attribution is an excellent method to illustrate two important points. It is a reminder that every sphere on the Tree of Life is an emanation from the spheres proceeding it, and that Kether and Yesod both represent the element of Air. While it is true that these points are very important, the method of illustrating this correlation has, in my experience as a teacher, confused the beginner. I feel Crowley's placement lacks explanation, which makes the subject too complex for many ground-level students of the Qabalah. Since we are far from experiencing a shortage of Egyptian or Greek deities, I have used the gods I have employed in my Qabalistic dealings.

Students familiar with the Qabalah and the Tree of Life will easily understand the significance of Crowley's dual placement. It is sufficient to say that all male gods of any particular hierarchy are expressions of the male supreme god of that particular pantheon; the same is true with the female gods. In other words, they represent the archetypal male and female deities. In the case of Kether, from which all gods illustrated below it have emanated, gender is moot point since at Kether both male and female qualities of the one god are merged.

I have simplified what follows, and am using the gods listed to illustrate the Qabalistic formula to the reader. Please don't forget that this is my Qabalah; you should strive to personalize your own, according to your understanding and feelings of mythology – you will find the effort very rewarding. Other mythological study is advised.

The models that follow are illustrative. Please keep in mind that the following Qabalistic placement represents one among many of possibilities. The number next to the god's name represents the sephirah it corresponds to.

The Egyptian Gods

1 – PTAH

Ptah is the Egyptian God of Memphis, defender of craftsmen and artists. He is usually represented as a mummy. He is credited with the invention of the arts, and was a metalworker and architect. He was usually associated with the bull Apis.

It was believed that Ptah, in the form of a heavenly fire, impregnated a virgin calf and from her, he himself was born again in the form of a black bull, which the priests recognized by a series of mysterious marks. His forehead had to bear a white triangle, while on his backside was a figure of a vulture with outstretched wings, on his right hip a crescent moon, on his tongue a scarab beetle, and finally, the hairs on his tail had to be double.

Normally, this lucky bull was allowed to live in the temples erected in his honor, and was cared for by the priests until his natural death.

2 – THOTH

Thoth was identified by the Greeks as Hermes, the Messenger of The Gods. He is the Egyptian champion of science, literature, wisdom, and invention, spokesman of Gods, and keeper of The Record. Originally represented with a head of an ibis, Thoth at times liked to appear as a dog-headed ape.

In Hermopolis, Thoth was believed to have hatched the World Egg. When he first sang, the sound of his voice created four gods and four goddesses; for this reason, Hermopolis was called Khnum, meaning "The City of Eight." These eight unknown gods continued the world's creation by word and song. He helped Isis restore Osiris, and sustained the Child Horus. He became the judge of Horus and Set, sentencing Set to return the kingdom to his nephew. As he had been Osiris's minister, he likewise served Horus in this capacity. Thoth was endowed with knowledge and wisdom. He invented the arts and sciences, arithmetic, surveying, geometry, astronomy, music, medicine, string and wind instruments; but most importantly, he invented writing.

Some texts allude to his marriage with Maat (the Goddess of Truth and Justice).

3 – Isis

Wife of Osiris, mother of Horus, and the first daughter of Geb and Nut, Isis was chosen by her oldest brother, Osiris, to share the throne. She created marriage, taught women to grow corn and weave clothes, and taught men to cure disease.

When her husband was killed by their brother Set, she cut off her hair, destroyed her clothing, and searched the Nile for her husband's body. Upon finding her beloved's coffin, she bathed it in tears and brought it back to Egypt, where she made love to his lifeless body to conceive Horus.

Set, upon hearing the news, took possession of the body, and to assure himself of his brother's permanent annihilation, he cut Osiris into fourteen pieces, which he then scattered throughout Egypt. The determined Isis searched and recovered every piece of her husband's body, except for the phallus, which had been devoured by a crab.

She pieced Osiris back together and performed, for the first time in Egyptian history, the rites of embalmment, which gave her murdered god-husband eternal life. She was assisted by Anubis, Thoth, and her son Horus, whom she had conceived by copulation with her husband's corpse. She raised Horus for the day when he could avenge his father's death.

Isis was a powerful magician; she represents the rich plain of Egypt, made fertile by the annual flooding of the Nile (where her husband's phallus is said to reside), which is separated from her by the desert of Set.

She is represented wearing a headdress consisting of a disk set between two feathers or horns; at times, however, she appears with a woman's body and a cow's head, which identifies her with Hathoor. It is believed that Horus grew enraged at Isis for attempting to discourage his revenge on Set (after all, Set *was* Isis's brother) cut off her head. Thoth then gave her the head of a cow.

4 – Amoun

Amoun bore the title "Little King of The Gods." Hence, the Greeks likened him unto Zeus. Amoun was the God of expedition and discovery. He appeared in human form wearing a crown fashioned of two tall feathers, and at times he is depicted with a head of a ram. The goose was his sacred animal. (Compare this with the story of Zeus and Leda). Amoun was a phallic god, representing the forces of creation and reproduction.

At one time, all men proclaimed to be his children; all other gods were destroyed. (It is interesting to note that this attempt at monotheism was occurring simultaneously in Asia, where the Syrians worshiped Adonis and the Jews, Adoni.) He grants his followers with long life and makes them powerful over their enemies with a magical fluid called "sa".

5 – Horus

Horus is the Latin name for the Greek Horos, and the Egyptian Hoor. Originally a solar God, and therefore identified with Apollo, Horus is usually represented as a falcon; other times, he is represented as a hawk. He was a popular god and one of the most worshiped; the Egyptians pantheon defines over twenty Horuses. It was believed that the Moon and the Sun were the eyes of Horus, and so he was called *Haroeris*, which means "Horus of the two eyes."

His story was told to explain the phenomenon of the rising and setting Sun; the never ending battle against his brother Set illustrated the travels of the Sun when it could not be seen. Since the Sun always rises, he was given the title *Hor Nubit*, which means "Horus the Vanquisher of Set."

We see him identified with Ra, the Sun God, and as *Harakhtes*, which means "Horus of The Horizon." He was so often identified with the Sun that for a time he was united with Ra, and they were worshiped as one God named *Ra-Harakhte*.

To differentiate Horus the brother of Set, from Horus the Sun-God, he was referred to as *Hor-Sa-Iset*, which means "Horus The Son of Isis," or "Horus the Younger."

When he was young, he was called *Harpakhrad*, which means "Horus the Infant," whom the Greeks called *Harpokrates*. In this form, he was usually depicted with his thumb pressed against his lips.

The famous Egyptian Sphinx was carved out in his honor; the name of the Sphinx, *Hor-M-Akhet*, means "Horus Who Is On The Horizon," and suggests the diurnal resurrection of the Sun.

6 – RA

The Egyptian name for sun, Ra, means "creator." He was principally worshiped at Heliopolis, where his priests believed he first manifested as a stone in the form of an obelisk – a petrified ray of the sun.

Before manifesting in Heliopolis, Ra rested under the name "Atum in the ocean," where he lay with his eyes shut in order to avoid being extinguished by the waters. One day he rose out from the abyss, enclosed within a lotus, shinning gloriously in the Egyptian sky.

From Ra came Shu and Tefnut, from whom came Geb and Nut (Nuit), from whom came Osiris and Isis.

The story was told, in Heliopolis, of a time when men plotted against Ra, who in a fit of rage threw his Divine Eye at his enemies. This eye took the form of Hathoor, who took revenge against the guilty. (See Hathoor/Sekhmet).

His distaste for men caused him to withdraw from the reach of his potential enemies on the back of Nuit, who had turned herself into a cow for the event. And this, so it was taught in Heliopolis, is the reason that Ra dwells in the skies.

Ra was born every morning as a child, who aged throughout the day to die an old man at sunset.

He is represented as a child on a lotus, a man upon whose head is a solar disk fashioning the uraeus, or as a man with a ram's head. Other times he is personified as a man with the head of a falcon under the name Ra-ha-rakhte, The God of Heliopolis.

7 – HATHOOR\SEKHMET

There seem to have been two faces to Hathoor, and we will discuss them both to shed light on the qualities of Netzach, which may appear at times to be at odds. These metaphors are also expressed in the Greek mythoi that pertain to this sephirah – the stories of Aphrodite and Athena. Aphrodite, the goddess of love, and

Athena, who is not only the goddess of war and battle (which represents the strength and drive of that love), but also of the arts.

(Hathoor for devotion and artistic qualities, and Sekhmet for the passionate fire that consumes – Lust. By lust, I mean the creative quality in the mind that feeds the imagination in the ultra-creative artisan.)

The Greeks identified Hathoor as Aphrodite. Some Egyptian texts indicate that it was Hathoor who created the world, even the Sun.

Sometimes she appears as the daughter of Ra and the wife of Horus. She is depicted as a cow, or as a cow-headed woman, although in some instances she is shown simply as a woman with cow's ears and horns.

She was the goddess of joy and love, and she protected women. She was the Lady of dance, music, and song, and later became the goddess of weaving. Her temples were described as being homes of intoxication and palaces of enjoyment.

Like Anubis, she was oftentimes charged with the pleasant duty of transporting the dead on her back to the afterlife.

Sekhmet means "The Powerful," and is the name given to Hathoor when she threw herself against those plotting against Ra. In this aspect, she is depicted as a woman with the head of a lioness.

Her attack upon men was so zealous that Ra feared the destruction of the entire human race. Ra begged her to cease, and when she refused he placed 7,000 bottles of a magical potion made from beer and pomegranate juice on the battleground.

Sekhmet's thirst for human blood was so great that she devoured the red liquid and became too drunk to continue killing; this is how Ra saved the human race. In her honor, on the day of Hathoor, thousands of jugs of the potion are brewed. She was often worshiped as the goddess of brewing.

8 – ANUBIS

The Greeks identified Anubis with Hermes. He is either represented as a black jackal, or a black-skinned man with a jackal's head.

He was the god of embalming and the companion of souls. He is the son of Nephthys and Osiris. At birth, he was abandoned by his mother and found by his aunt Isis who, feeling no jealousy toward her husband's affair with her sister, raised Anubis as her own.

When Osiris was murdered by Set, Anubis helped Isis bury him, and this is when Anubis invented mummification to protect Osiris from decay. He presides over funerals and directs the dead to the afterworld.

9 – Shu

Ra created Shu without means of woman. It is said that Ra, displeased with the union of Nuit, the sky goddess, and Geb, the earth god, ordered Shu to slip between the couple and elevate the body of Nuit to separate them. This action was responsible for creating the space between the earth and the sky – air.

Appropriately, Shu means "he who holds up," and Shu is the god of air. The pillars of the Tree of Life are referred to as "The Pillars of Shu." He is always depicted as a man wearing a feather upon his head.

It is said that he became king of the earth, which he ruled until he retreated to the skies during a violent windstorm that lasted *nine* days – the number of the sephirah to which he corresponds.

10 – Osiris

Osiris began his career as a nature god and represented the spirit of vegetation, which perishes with the harvest but rises again in the blooming grain. He was the son of Geb and Nuit, and was born in Thebes.

Despite what Ra thought of the union of his parents, he received Osiris joyfully and made him the heir to his throne. When Osiris became king of Egypt, he took his sister Isis as his wife.

It is taught that Osiris instructed men in the agricultural arts and showed them how to produce grain, make bread, and how to use grapes to make wine. He was a gentle god, and it was with kindness that he civilized the world.

His brother Set was so jealous of his power that he killed Osiris, much like the biblical story of Cain and Able.

Isis used her magical powers, and with the assistance of Thoth, Anubis, and Horus, brought Osiris back to life.

The corn is sacred to Osiris, and he is considered one and indivisible with the Nile, which rises and falls, making Egypt fertile.

He is pictured with a green face, and with arms folded across his chest, with which he holds the scourge and scepter, emblems of his sovereignty.

The Greek Gods

1 – IACCHUS

Ironically, if one looks for references to this god, one will inevitably be led to Dionysus. In fact, very little is known of Iacchus outside of the fact that he *was* confused with Dionysus, and later treated as the same god.

Crowley's first choice for Kether appears to have been Zeus, and he states in his comments that the Zeus of Kether is a different quality than the Zeus at Yesod.

The reason I prefer Iacchus as a representative of Kether is that the transliteration of his name begins with the Hebrew letter Yod, the source for the rest of the Hebrew letters. This alludes nicely to the fact that all of the sephiroth are emanations or expressions which originate from Kether.

Many poorly prepared magicians have confused Tiphareth with Kether in their meditations, and as a result, one sees many mediocre practitioners boasting they have crossed the abyss. In the Christian religion, Christ belongs to the realm of Tiphareth, yet the uninitiated perceive Jesus to be the "one god," a title which obviously belongs to Kether. The Greek myth of Dionysus comes closer to the truth of the relationship between Tiphareth and Kether.

I have therefore preferred to use Iacchus for Kether, the god which was later confused with Dionysus (whom I have placed at Tiphareth) in the Greek mysteries. Iacchus is a higher form of Dionysus, just as Kether is a higher form of Tiphareth.

Again, Iacchus was often confused with Dionysus, and in the Elysian Mysteries was considered to be the son of Zeus and Demeter. He was a fertility god whose function was very similar to that of Bacchus. He was worshiped by farmers and others whose livelihoods depended on the fruit of the vine.

2 – URANUS

Uranus was a sky god who was crowned with the stars. He was the father of Aphrodite, and was both son and husband of Gaea, "the deep breasted," who seems to have been an early Greek conception of the physical earth. There is an early tradition that states that Uranus was the father of the Muses.

He and his mother-wife created the first humanoid race, known as the Titans. They later conceived the Cyclopes and three monsters called the Hecatoncheires, whom he despised so much he shut them up within the depths of the earth.

This move enraged Gaea and caused her to plan revenge against her husband-son. Using steel she drew forth from her bosom, she created a sickle of legendary sharpness.

She tried to recruit her children to carry out the gruesome deed, but all of them were stricken with horror except one – Cronus.

At night while Uranus slept, Cronus took the sickle, castrated him and cast his genitals into the sea. The blood of his genitals mingled with the ocean water, creating a white foam that floated on top of the waves, and from this foam Aphrodite was born.

When his blood fell upon the earth, the Titan Cyclopes and Hecatoncheires escaped their prisons in the bowels of the earth and attacked Olympus.

The gods stood fast, but a divination disclosed that only a mortal could cause the offspring of Uranus to fall. This mortal's name was Heracles, and he, with the help of Athena and Hera, finished the monsters off.

Of the Titans that Uranus had fathered, only one was held in high regard; in fact, Zeus married her at the beginning of his reign. Her name was Themis. Later, when Zeus married Hera, Themis served Zeus as advisor. Hera never displayed any jealousy towards her, probably due to the fact that it was Themis who had first given Hera the cup of nectar that made her immortal.

3 – DEMETER

Demeter was the mother of Persephone, or Kore, who represented the earth. Like her daughter, Demeter represented fertility, and as we shall see later, with the abduction her daughter she became the goddess of maternal loss.

She was first employed as the goddess of the fertile soil; wheat and barley were sacred to her, and she was worshiped as a deity of fruits and vegetables. She quickly adapted the essence of the meaning of her name, "Earth Mother," which illustrates rather nicely the relationship between Binah and Malkuth.

She was credited with the creation and dispensation of marital law. Her temples were often hidden in the woods, perhaps to keep away unwanted individuals who might have otherwise participated in the orgies practiced there.

She was the daughter of Cronus and Rhea. We will soon see how she attempted to escape the advances of Poseidon by turning herself into a mare. She was very beautiful, and it was not long before Zeus fixed his sights on her. By Zeus, she conceived Kore.

The primary incident that contributed to Demeter's grief over the loss of her daughter was the revelation that Zeus, the father of Kore, had willingly given their child to Hades, lord of the underworld. He probably did this in order to ensure a consistent harvest.

Demeter was so distraught that she left Olympus to walk upon the earth with the mortals. It was perhaps her disgust towards the insensitivity of gods of Olympus that prompted her to anoint, purify, and consecrate a mortal child a god.

She might have succeeded in seating a mortal in Olympus had the mother of the child not panicked when Demeter tried to consecrate the child on the flames of a fire. Had she succeeded, the Greek myths might have included yet another man that became a god, and perhaps we would have seen this infant, whose name was Demophoon, occupying the sphere of Tiphareth.

She taught mortals how to work the soil and use oxen to pull the plow across the fields, techniques that her students quickly spread to the rest of civilization.

So bitter at the loss of Kore was Demeter that she caused the earth to hold back its fruit; mankind was about to perish from hunger. Zeus, wanting to spare humanity, attempted to sway her, but she refused unless she could see her daughter.

Zeus sent Hermes to the underworld to find Kore (who was now known as Persephone) and return her to her mother. Hades agreed, but swayed Persephone to eat from a pomegranate. Demeter's cries for joy were stifled by the news that Persephone had eaten the deadly fruit, because doing so meant that she would have to return to the underworld. This is reminiscent of the Biblical myth of Eve and the forbidden fruit.

Zeus, having been touched by the tears of Demeter, ruled that Persephone would live with her husband Hades in the underworld for one third of the year; she would live the rest of the year with her mother.

As a result, the fertility of the soil was restored, and it was covered with leaves and flowers. It was a good harvest. Demeter was able to see her daughter regularly and returned to her seat on Olympus; Hades was able to retain his wife, and everyone seems to have been satisfied.

And it was thus that the people of Greece were spared a great famine. They rationalized the fall and winter by Kore's descent into the underworld, and the spring with her union with her mother.

4 – Poseidon

Poseidon was the god of the seas, and was considered one of the great gods of Olympus. Scholars believe him to be a much older god even than Zeus, and that his trident was, perhaps, the symbol of the thunderbolt. His early career was as the god of earthquakes, and later he confined his dominion to the sea. Later still, not being satisfied with the immense ocean, Poseidon controlled lakes, rivers, and streams.

Horses, bulls, and springs were sacred to Poseidon; in fact, during certain holidays, black bulls were thrown into to the waves in his honor. He is said to have created the horse with his mighty trident.

Poseidon was one of many children eaten by his father Cronus, and was freed when Zeus poisoned Cronus and made him throw up.

There were three great gods at Olympus, and the dominion of the universe was divided between them. Zeus got the heavens, Poseidon the seas, and Hades the underworld.

When the gods went to war against the Giants, Poseidon split whole mountains with his trident and caused them to slide into the waters; this and similar actions caused him to be identified with the islands and the corrosive results of moving water on the land. He symbolizes the rage of the sea, and all of the inhabitants of lands near the sea paid homage to this mighty god.

Poseidon attempted to spread his dominion from the oceans over to the lands, and this put him competition with many other gods. In the end, he had little to show for his efforts but a little island called Calauria.

He enjoyed many women, and like Zeus, he used his magick to conquer those that attempted to escape him. He went after Demeter, who turned into a mare to outrun him, but much to her dismay Poseidon took her by turning himself into a stallion. From this union, Arion was born – a horse who could speak, and whose right feet were human.

To seduce Medusa, he changed himself into a bird. Everything might have been fine had he chosen a different site to fulfill his sexual desires, but the couple ended up in the temple of Athena, who was so outraged at the desecration of her holy space that she turned Medusa's hair into serpents.

Poseidon asked to marry Aphrodite, who represented the feminine and creative aspects of the sea, but she declined the invitation and tried to flee him by hiding herself in Atlas.

She was discovered by a dolphin and brought back to Poseidon; they were then married and ruled together. She is often pictured with Poseidon in his chariot, where she holds Poseidon's trident as a sign of her power and authority. She was a tolerant wife, and endured her partner's many affairs.

There is only one account of intolerance, which began when Poseidon became deeply infatuated by a nymph of exceptional beauty. Aphrodite poisoned a pond where Poseidon's mistress bathed, turning her into a hideous monster.

As in the case of Zeus, the limited scope of this treatise makes it impossible to list all of his affairs and offspring.

5 – ARES

Ares comes from a Greek root which means 'destroy.' He is pictured as a heavily bearded man, or as a younger man fashioning a toga while holding a spear and wearing a helmet.

He was the son of Hera and Zeus. His virtuous attributions were courage and valor; his vices were rage, carnage, and blind fury. He was the god of war. He was feared and disliked equally by mortal and god; Zeus thought of him as wicked.

He would show himself on the battlefield killing on both sides with his four companions – Deimos, which means Fear; Phobos, meaning Fright; Eris, which means Strife; and Enyo, who was the destroyers of cities. Ares appears to have enjoyed unwarranted violence.

In contrast, Athena, the goddess of war, possessed an even temper and unconditional courage, and because of this they often fought on opposite sides.

Ares once attacked Athena so ferociously that the thunderbolt of Zeus could not stop his spear. In defense, Athena hit Ares on the neck with a huge black stone that brought Ares to the ground. Athena proved that intelligence and chivalry would always triumph over the savage in matters of war.

Ares even engaged in battle with Hercules, who defeated him; he might have been killed had Zeus not interfered by dropping a lightning bolt between them.

Contrary to how he is usually portrayed, he rarely won battles, perhaps because his uncontrollable temper interfered with his intellectual capacities.

One may wonder why Athena, who was truly courageous on the battlefield, might not best represent Geburah, but she was primarily identified with arts such as weaving, architecture, and sculpting. She also remained a virgin, and perhaps her placement on the sephirah that represents the force and strength of Kundalini is seen as inappropriate. Crowley identified her as a goddess of Wisdom; and because "she springs fully armed from the brain of Zeus" (which he places at Kether), he puts her at Chokmah.

6 – APOLLO/DIONYSUS

I invoke Apollo for matters dealing with health or music, and Dionysus for things pertaining to spiritual strength.

Apollo was a sun god, and it was the sun's influence over the harvest that made him an important god to the Greeks. Like the physical sun whose rays can both restore and consume, so was Apollo depicted as healer and destroyer. The powers of divination were attributed to him, as it was believed that Zeus spoke through him.

He began his career as a shepherd god, and we shall soon see where his transition to a musical god took place. It was believed by the Greeks that when a building was erected, it was Apollo himself who laid the foundation.

He is usually represented beardless, with long curly hair that fell to his shoulders. He was seen most often naked, and the Greeks depicted him as the epitome of beauty. The bow, crook, and lyre are attributed to him; the vulture, hawk, swan, wolf, and serpent are his sacred animals. His divine plants are the laurel, palm, and olive.

Apollo was the offspring of Zeus and Leto, who was a victim of Hera's rage. It seems that when Leto became pregnant, she sought refuge on the earth in order to give birth. She finally found a place where she could deliver, but since Hera had sworn that Leto would never give birth in the light, Poseidon covered the island like a dome and darkened it. After Apollo was born, the name of the island became Delos, which means "brilliant."

So jealous was Hera that while the other gods rushed to the island to witness the birth, she detained Ilithya, the goddess of childbirth, causing Leto to suffer the pangs of birth for nine days. It is said that when Leto finally gave birth, the earth smiled beneath her feet, and the goddesses wept with joy. On this same occasion, she also gave birth to Apollo's sister, Artemis. When Apollo was a child, he was given nectar and sweet ambrosia, which caused him to instantly become an adult.

Again, we saw Hera's unbridled jealousy when she sent a female dragon called Python to devour Leto at the moment of Apollo's birth; the dragon could not reach Leto, thanks to Poseidon's watery dome.

Armed with arrows forged by Hephaestus, the blacksmith god, Apollo killed Python, who incidentally happened to be the same serpent who suckled Typhon. Apollo represented all children of Greece.

There is a curious account of a musical battle that took place between Apollo and Pan. Apollo would have unanimously won, had the king of Phryga not voted in Pan's favor. The victorious Apollo punished the king by giving him the ears of an ass. Pan was flogged, and was later hung on the entrance of a cave.

Despite his beauty, several of his loves resisted him. When he tried to seduce Daphne, the beautiful virgin, she called upon Gaea to help escape Apollo; the earth opened up underneath her feet and Daphne was swallowed up. A laurel tree popped up where she had stood, and this is how the laurel tree became sacred to Apollo. He had many children. One of his sons, Asclepius, became the god of medicine; another son, named Idmon, could see the future.

Apollo seems to have been a newer form or expression of an older solar deity named Helios.

DIONYSUS – Zeus saw a beautiful mortal named Semele picking grapes. He seduced her and she became pregnant. One day, while Zeus visited with Semele, the jealous Hera disguised herself as one of Semele's nurses, and convinced her to ask Zeus to show himself to her in his Olympian splendor.

Zeus showed himself to her, and she was burned up by the light which emanated from him. Hera had imagined that the unborn child would also perish by fire, but ivy sprang quickly between Zeus and the unborn child.

Zeus picked up the infant and hid it in his own thigh until it was developed enough to endure the outside world. With the help of Ilithyia, the goddess of childbirth, he withdrew the child Dionysus. Zeus then entrusted the sister of Semele, Ino, with the care of the child.

There is another story which states that Cadmus, the father of Semele, was so enraged at his daughter's promiscuity that he locked her into a chest and threw it into the water. When the chest washed ashore, it was found by Ino and opened. Semele was dead, but the child Dionysus was alive.

Hera continued trying to gratify her lust for vengeance. She struck Ino and her husband with madness. Zeus came to the rescue of the child once again by changing the child into a kid (goat), and ordered Hermes to deliver him to the nymphs of Nysa. The Satyrs, Nymphs, and the Muses educated him.

When he grew to an adult, Dionysus discovered the secret of the grape, and made wine. He spread throughout the world educating humans on the art of winemaking.

Pirates, not knowing he was something of a god-man, kidnapped him. While he was being held in the chambers of their ship, he caused a vine to grow out of a barrel of wine and crush the sail and mast; he then turned himself into a lion. The pirates jumped ship, and as they hit the water Dionysus turned them into dolphins.

The king of the land called Thrace turned against Dionysus, and the young god sought shelter in the depths of the sea. He then caused the land of the king to become sterile and yield no fruit.

His dialog with the mortals he encountered while attempting to convert them into his cult was very similar to the biblical Jesus. The poets and philosophers wrote about him profusely, and quoted him making profound statements that allude to his connection to the gods: "That which you do to me you also do to the Gods," etc.

Dionysus is represented wearing an Asian robe and a crown of ivy upon his head. Men and women alike usually adored him, and huge orgies followed the worship.

He was a jealous god. When his cult spread throughout the land, he punished people who would not submit to the orgies associated with his worship. His method of revenge appears to have been driving people to insanity (perhaps a drinking disorder), and soon nobody denied the divinity of Dionysus.

After having duly established his cult, he descended into the bowels of the earth in search of his mother, Semele. Upon finding her, he changed her name to Thyone and brought her to Olympus to live with the gods.

Some historians believe that his wife was the moon-goddess Bendis. One account describes his murder by a Titan who put his parts into a cauldron. Athena retrieved the still beating heart, and from this Zeus reconstructed Dionysus. As a result of this account, Dionysus underwent a transformation in the collective consciousness of the people. He was no longer associated with orgies and wine, but became a god of resurrection, identified with the sun.

7 – APHRODITE

Aphrodite was the goddess of Love, and the lover of Ares, the god of War. Curiously, the name Aphrodite appears be of oriental origin. She began her career as a goddess of nature, and later (for reasons we will soon see) represented love in its virtuous form as well as its most profane. For example, Aphrodite Porne ruled over lust and was worshiped by prostitutes. Aphrodite Genetrix was the goddess of marriage and was treasured by widows and single women, who prayed to her to help them find husbands.

Her statues adorned the Greek bathhouses, and often depicted her armed with a spear and wearing a helmet. Some scholars think that this pose reflects her relationship with Ares, but it is most likely that the warrior aspect of Aphrodite is a carryover of the Babylonian war goddess, Ishstar.

Her birth was rather fascinating. It seems that Cronus, following the orders of his mother Gaea, castrated his father Uranus, and threw his genitals into the sea. This produced a white foam, from which Aphrodite was born.

She floated on the foam until she reached the coast of Cyprus. She was then taken to the dwelling place of the gods, where everyone was touched by her great beauty.

She was a considerate and caring goddess whose great devotion and sense of duty to all of her devotees drove her to the battlefield, only to be defeated. Zeus, who told her that her nature was to love and to leave the matters of war to better suited gods, consoled her.

She had been the wife of Hephaestus, a blacksmith god associated with the creative fire that enabled artists and blacksmiths to manifest mechanical ideas. Because he had a limp that caused him to zigzag as he walked, he was also identified with lightning.

Aphrodite, unsympathetic of her husband's handicap, soon took a liking to the energetic and good looking Ares. Helios, after getting wind of the lovers' actions, reported their affair to Hephaestus, who made a trap designed to catch the lovers in the act.

He forged a metal net so slender it was transparent, and so secure it could not be damaged. He then placed the net over his bed, where the lovers reportedly met, and told Aphrodite he would be out of town.

When Ares saw Hephaestus leaving, he convinced Aphrodite to meet with him. While they slept, Hephaestus sprang his trap and called for the gods, whose laughter awakened Ares and Aphrodite. The couple was ashamed. Ares consented to retire to the mountains of Thrace; Aphrodite fled to the island of Cypress. From this union, Aphrodite gave birth to a daughter named Harmonia. [5,6,7, on Tree of Life]

There is a touching story of a mortal sculptor named Pygmalion, whose love for Aphrodite was so strong that other women disgusted him. He secluded himself and sculpted a beautiful woman from stone. Then one day, Pygmalion made an ivory statue of a woman so beautiful he fell in love with it. He caressed and kissed the statue, and Aphrodite, moved by his loneliness and devotion, caused the statue to return his kisses by giving her life.

Aphrodite was equally stern and capable of mischief. When displeased, she was known to torment mortals by causing nymphomania in the women of her enemies.

For a time, she had been the lover of Hermes, and from their union was born a boy called Hermaphroditus. To keep the secret of his birth, she entrusted the boy to nymphs who brought him up in the woods, where hunting became his favorite pursuit.

Stumbling upon a beautiful clear lake, he was confronted by a nymph who was immediately stricken by his beauty. She attempted to lure the young man him into the water with her, but failed.

The stubborn nymph, enraged that Hermaphroditus had declined her invitation, called up to the gods and petitioned them to bring them together. From that day forwards, their bodies were united as one body displaying both sexes. To paraphrase a teacher of mine: Be careful what you ask for... you might get it.

Perhaps Aphrodite's most significant offspring was Eros. Because he maintains qualities of all three gods, no one can agree upon whether his father was Ares, Hermes, or Zeus. He was a zealous servant and had wings, like Hermes. We see equal portions of Aphrodite and Ares in him, since fashioned he a bow and arrows with which he stirred the hearts of men and women. He was both charming and cruel, like Zeus.

Aphrodite was prone to fits of jealousy, especially when she felt threatened by the beauty of other women. She was so envious of Psyche that she enlisted Eros to pierce her heart with an arrow, a move designed to make Psyche fall in love with Death. Instead, Eros accidentally pierced his own finger with the arrow intended for Psyche, and when he looked at her, fell madly in love.

8 – Hermes

Hermes is often represented as an athletic young man wearing winged leather sandals and hat. In his hands he holds a winged staff around which two serpents are coiled – the caduceus.

Hermes was the son of Zeus, and from the day he was born displayed prankster-like qualities.

The young Hermes was a very mobile god. One day, he escaped the confines of his cradle and climbed over the neighboring mountains, where he spotted a herd of cattle that had been entrusted to Apollo. He separated the herd into two, and drove one half of them into the night. So cunning was Hermes that he made the cows walk backward so their hoof marks would confuse anyone choosing to follow their direction. He covered his own feet with twigs to avoid leaving footprints.

He hid the cows in a cave, after which he took out two of the fattest and roasted them over a fire he had started by rubbing two laurel sticks together. He divided the meat into twelve parts and offered one part to each of the twelve gods. He then returned to his cradle.

Much dismayed by the disappearance of no less than fifty cows, Apollo used divination to determine what had occurred. When Hermes denied the charges, the angry Apollo seized him and took Hermes to the Tribunal of Zeus. Hermes was instructed to return the heifers.

To appease Apollo, Hermes gave him a musical instrument composed of an emptied tortoise shell with seven sheep gut strings stretched over it, which gave a beautiful sound when plucked. This was the birth of the lyre.

In exchange, Apollo gave him the caduceus, and put him in charge of the herd. Such a strong bond was created between the two that Hermes delivered several of Apollo's offspring. This is how Hermes became the protector of herds, and Apollo became the god of music.

Hermes was well liked, despite his occasional schemes. He was so well liked by Hera that she overlooked the fact that he was the result of an affair between Zeus and Maia, and she often allowed Hermes to feed from her own breasts.

Hermes was a valiant god, and fought many wars. He killed the giant Hippolytus, who did not see him coming because Hermes wore the helmet of Hades, which enables the wearer to become invisible.

9 – Zeus

Zeus has a fascinating and prolific history. Similar to Shu, Zeus was the god of air, wind, clouds, rain, and lightning. He was considered all knowing and became the source of all divination.

As a ruler, he was stern with the wicked but displayed understanding and tenderness toward the vulnerable. Apollo was the prophet to which he communicated the Law.

Because he was the god of air, he was worshiped at all high places, especially Mt. Olympus. The rustling of the leaves of his sacred tree, the oak, was believed to be the voice of Zeus himself.

He is usually depicted as a fully bearded man wearing a golden mantle, and on his head he bore an olive wreath. In his left hand, he held a scepter, on which rested an eagle, and in his right hand, he held the lightning bolt.

Perhaps his strongest association with Yesod is his sexual appetite. He first married Metis, whose name means Wisdom. Fearing that their offspring would be wiser than he, he swallowed Metis as she was about to give birth – a move which proved to work in his favor, as then he possessed all wisdom within him.

His next wife was Themis, who represented the laws of social and religious order. From their union came Horae (the seasons), Eunomia (wise legislation), Dike (justice), Eirent (peace), and the Fates. Themis was eventually replaced, but remained as an adviser to her husband.

He then married Mnemosyne, who gave birth to nine daughters

after Zeus spent nine evenings with her. These daughters were called the Muses. Nine is the number of Yesod.

Zeus had a passionate crush on Demeter, but she ignored his advances. Not to be outdone or ruin a perfect record, he changed himself into a bull, and raped her. This is how he became the father of Kore.

Zeus seems to have relied on his ability to become an animal many times, in order to satisfy his sexual desires.

Hera, one of Zeus's many wives, was driven to jealousy, and kept quite busy keeping up with Zeus while punishing the goddesses and mortal women he copulated with.

Perhaps one of the most significant Qabalistically important of his offspring were Apollo and Artemis, twins whose mother was a titaness called Leto. His most remembered seduction is his union to the mortal Leda, which he accomplished by turning himself into a beautiful swan.

His sexual adventures are too numerous for the scope of this treatise. I think he was a fascinating model as far as gods go, and would encourage further research to the reader who wishes to keep score.

10 - PERSEPHONE

Persephone was known by her parents, Demeter and Zeus, as Kore. She became Persephone when while picking flowers she was seized by Hades, the Lord of The Underworld, who was invisible while wearing his helmet. They then plunged into the Underworld in his chariot.

While the significance of the name Persephone is unclear, some scholars believe that her title is derived from two words that together mean "She who destroys light."

Demeter, stricken with grief at her daughter's abduction, was successful in bargaining with Hades, convincing him to allow Persephone to spend the spring and summer months with her parents. In other words, Persephone symbolizes the two most prominent phases of nature. The spring, which causes things grow, is explained by the time she spends upon the earth. The autumn, when the growing season is over, is symbolized by her decent into The Underworld.

The bat is sacred to her because of her association with the Underworld. The pomegranate is attributed to her fertile aspects.

The Thelemic Gods

What is a Thelemite? This is a loaded question. To try to answer it would be to invoke the wrath of Thelemites whose views are not included in the reply. There is no single answer, because there are as many variables as there are people. I have known Thelemites who have reconciled Thelema with Christianity, Buddhism, Islam, Judaism, etc. This philosophy speaks to everyone individually, as it should. On the other hand, I believe that the question deserves more respect than the usual generic answer one gets: "A Thelemite is a person who has accepted the Word of The Law." I will attempt to satisfy the reader while avoiding disrespect to individuals with contrasting experiences, by making this simple statement: Thelema is a universal philosophy or way of life. It encompasses every other philosophy and way of life. Hence, it would be impossible to write about it because defining it completely would be to reduce its infinite power, influence, and evolutionary importance. Any attempt to do so would be a miserable failure on my part; and anyone making such a claim is insinuating that the philosophy has been transcended. I make no such claims.

Those of us who consider ourselves Thelemites are willing to accept responsibility for doing our Will. The exceptions to the rule, of course, have conveniently interpreted The Law as a license to do what they want, with little regard for the rights of other individuals.

There is a price to pay for living life on your own terms – namely that in your efforts to find your true path, you may at times experience a reality at odds with your inner nature. To find your place within the Universe, you must interpret the experience in a way that will lead you closer to your own path. Should you end up on a path that is not congenial with your true nature, you will suffer the consequences.

One who subscribes to the Christian Myth might equate this suffering with Hell: a separation from God. In the Thelemic context, it means that the experience has not led one closer to Knowledge and Conversation with the Holy Guardian Angel. Jesus had attained this awareness – communion with God. In its efforts to control its adherents, modern day Christianity has turned Jesus into the world's Holy Guardian Angel by insisting that anyone who does not pray through him will not find salvation.

While it is true that one of the main functions of the art and science of magick is to bring to a better understanding of our Selves, we must keep in mind that experience is the teacher. Much of finding our True Will is trial and error; we are in darkness, seeking the light. Perhaps this is why our Thelemic Gods encourage us to experience every conceivable combination of possibilities to find our place in the scheme of things. The contrast is easily seen in conventional religion. For some reason or another (one consideration being the myth of original sin), individuals are made to believe that they are unworthy of God's mercy. Not having this approval from God means that the follower will undoubtedly be punished in Hell. In other words, the myth that one will not be held accountable for his actions until after his incarnation has ended is perpetuated. Forgiveness is so easy to obtain that, more often than not, the same sin is repeated many times. Sinners feel confident when repeating the crime, since they know they are exempt from the consequences of their actions because their God forgives them.

A Thelemite accepts responsibility for his interference without invoking this forgiveness from some distant, exterior God, but is willing to face, endure, and answer to the result of his ignorance. Individual responsibility is a key factor, and one among many. Those who adhere to the magnificent principles in its teachings are beacons for the Light that it contains – every single one, each reflecting a different glorious ray – each and every one, according to his ability to manifest that Light to the rest of the world. *Liber Al vel Legis*, or *The Book of The Law*, in the bibliography of this book, is a good place to start.

Once, as I often do, I explained Thelema as a religion, and then one of my students asked me to better define it by comparing it to modern day Christianity. At first, I was shocked and disappointed because I thought I had somehow confused my student and had led him to believe that there were very few differences between them. In retrospect, however, I realized that the concepts were in fact very similar – but when one scrutinizes them side by side, the differences are enormous.

As stated elsewhere, Crowley himself thought of Thelema as a religion, the true Christianity—modern Gnosticism.

Christianity attempts to describe the metaphor of man becoming God, and I believe (and it seems Crowley would have agreed) that to be the purpose of Christian Mysticism. Here we have a man named Jesus, who by suffering (transcendence through pain) became a God. I hold the opinion that this Jesus, or Christ, alludes to a personal experience and a place where an individual finds himself to be at one with and indivisible from God. I have a friend that illustrates the problem in conventional Christianity with an ironic story about human nature, as follows:

There were many Christians wandering through the desert, thirsty, many of them about to die of dehydration. After traveling for several days, they came upon a sign that read, "Water: one mile ahead." All but a few of them rushed to embrace the sign, thinking that the sign would save them. This is the nature of man. That one among us, a man among men, a mortal, would discover the deity within him (his Holy Guardian Angel) only to have his fellow men drop to their knees in worship of him, rather than attempt to achieve the same goal.

Also, it is easy for a person who has gained Knowledge and Conversation to suddenly decide that he is now an expert on how everybody can achieve the same task. This is a prevalent problem in most magical communities, and this can only (given enough time) become a personality cult much like Christianity is today – you are forbidden to take any other path than the one chosen for you by the Church. I find it strange that men would rather turn their backs on the path that is uniquely theirs to try the methods of others, only to fail, only to spend their whole lives following the footsteps of Jesus, Mohammed, Buddha, Mathers, or Crowley. The concept that anyone would execute any form of prayer, yoga, ritual, or devotion for any other reason than to develop his own unique methods for attaining Christ Consciousness (which *is* after all Knowledge and Conversation) is beyond logic. Yet there are millions of people who do just that – many of them Thelemites.

Speaking from a theological perspective does not do much for the argument, either. Each person is unique and different from any person who has lived, is alive now, or will live in the future. How would it profit God if one were to attempt reaching It using the same method as Isaiah, when one is not Isaiah? How can one hope to accomplish this dangerous, long task using the methods at odds to one's own being? Does anybody *really* think that God expects us to be anything other than who we truly are? To me the question seems to be about sincerity. Do the masses find it easier to follow than to spend their lives finding their own paths through trial and error? You bet! Please do not get the idea that I am trying to throw mud at religious organizations. I'm not. I am a member of a few myself.

When we are drawn to particular beliefs or methods, we should find out why. Often, this realization alone will give us hints of who we truly are, and with much contemplation (and trial and error), we will be led to discovering new ways of doing things. Your religious leaders should honor the path you have chosen and should rejoice at your progress. If they disapprove, it may mean that you have taken an obvious wrong turn somewhere (in which case, they may be trying to help you avoid a pothole on the path), or it may mean that you have joined a cult. Generally, be aware of people or institutions who claim that they possess the only true way to salvation. Do the work of your predecessors, so that you may find the best way for you to manifest the glory of your own God. Do you think it is possible to find Joe by screaming out for Jill? I don't.

It is easy for people reading this to get the idea that there is one God, or many. I think both of these statements are true, and I also think arguing this point would be splitting hairs. *Liber AL* tells us what God is: Man. How we interpret this is up to each one of us.

Man is always trying to define the indefinable. For one man or one institution to claim that there is only one true way to godhood is an insult to the god they represent, because they have reduced Its omnipotence and omnipresence to the scope of their own minds. There is no reason to compare Thelema to Christianity to understand its beauty and complexity. The Qabalah unlocks all of the mysteries of religion, and yields its fruits to anyone who has eyes to see and ears to listen.

The placement of the following deities is only an example of many other possibilities. Please refer to *Liber AL vel Legis, The Book of The Law* to better understand the function of these deities and the logic for their placement. I consider myself a Thelemite, therefore, I will naturally try to use as many Thelemic deities, whether Egyptian or Greek, as I can in my personal Qabalah. My sources are listed in the bibliography. The cast I have chosen for placement on the Tree of Life includes Nuit, Hadit, Chaos, Babalon, Hoor-Par-Krat, Ra-Hoor-Khuit, Heru-Ra-Ha, The Scarlet Woman, Baphomet, Therion, and Ankh-Af-Na-Khonsu.

This is only an example I have devised to illustrate the placement of deities on the Tree of Life using archetypes congruent with Thelemic principles. I will state once again that the following is an outline or format, and like any other Qabalistic arrangement, it can be used as a guide for creating your own system of categorization. I have deliberately written little about these deities in hopes that you, the reader, may make your own decisions regarding their placement on the Tree of Life.

0 – NUIT: THE NEGATIVE VEILS OF EXISTENCE

Qabalistically, Nuit could represent the whole Tree, while Hadit could allude to any of the other sephiroth, depending on which truth we may be experiencing at any given time. And if we desire laziness to dictate the way we explore the Qabalah, we could put Nuit in Binah and Hadit at Chokmah. Since Nuit is "Infinite Space, and the Infinite Stars" (Crowley 2004), She fits rather nicely at Ain Soph.

Historically, She was the night sky, the Mother of the Gods who gave birth to Osiris and Isis, among others. She was both Mother and Daughter to Ra, who was angered when Nuit married Geb (her twin brother) in secrecy. Ra enlisted the God Shu to hold her belly away from Geb in an effort to separate the pair, and as a result the three Pillars on The Tree are often referred to as "The Pillars of Shu." Ra decreed that Nuit would not conceive in any month. Thoth, the Lord of Magick, took pity on Nuit as he had done for Isis, and came to Her rescue.

Thoth gambled on several occasions with the Moon until he had won 1/72 part of the Moon's light, with which he composed five new days. Since these five days did not traditionally belong to the Egyptian calendar of 360 days, this gave Nuit five days in which she could conceive. And it was thus that she bore Osiris, Isis, Horus, Set, and Nephthy.

Nuit also fits rather nicely in Da'ath (Knowledge), since it is mentioned several times that Her number is 11, and that the Universe (Infinite Space) can be contained within the human consciousness. If there were an 11th sephirah, Da'ath would certainly be it. I have adhered to the teachings of the *Sepher Yetzirah*, and have refrained from regarding Da'ath as a sephirah.

1 – HADIT: KETHER

Hadit's placement comes easy. Hadit and all of Its attributions fit perfectly in Kether.

While Nuit may arguably fit just as nicely at Kether, the idea of 'The

Crown' is a concept that alludes to The Ultimate Attainment, Union with God, hence better describing the principles of Hadit, Her lover. This is also evidenced by the fact that the Hebrew name Eheieh (I Am) is attributed to Kether, and alludes to the realization of the Self, which is embodied in Hadit.

2 – CHAOS: CHOKMAH

The conclusion behind placing Chaos and Babalon on Chokmah and Binah is obvious – the universe is a byproduct of the union of opposites. The union of Chokmah and Binah is the first such union taking place on the Tree. Chokmah is the archetypal Phallus and its seed contains all things possible, but not yet manifest: Chaos.

3 – BABALON: BINAH

Binah is the archetypal Yoni, and it is here that all things possible begin their development. Chaos possesses the seed, and Babalon the egg and womb of Existence.

It has been said that Order comes out of Chaos, but this is only so because Babalon provides a space for the development to occur.

To separate the qualities of Bright/Fertile from Dark/Sterile, Crowley attributed Civet as the incense used for invoking the Fertile aspects of Binah, and Myrrh for The Vision of Sorrow represented by Her sterility (Crowley 1986).

4 – HOOR-PAR-KRAT: CHESED

Appropriately, not much is said of Hoor-par-krat. He is the God of Silence, and is usually symbolized as a babe in a blue egg, holding His first finger to His lips in the Sign of Silence. In magick, Silence is equated with Love. Intuitively, I find He fits rather nicely at Chesed (Mercy), polarizing Ra-hoor-khuit.

5 – RA-HOOR-KHUIT: GEBURAH

One glance at Chapter III in *The Book of The Law* or Egyptian texts, and there won't be any doubt that Ra-hoor-khuit is a Martial God, and no other sephirah seems worthy of him. He is the representation of the violent surge of energy that occurs when raising the Kundalini, the Serpent coiled at the base of the spine. He alludes to the Will.

6 – HERU-RA-HA: TIPHARETH

Heru-ra-ha is the embodiment of the Holy Guardian Angel, and has therefore been placed in Tiphareth (Beauty), the place of Balance. It is a product of the union of Chaos (Chokmah) and Babalon (Binah). Here, the individuality of the parents is absorbed by the Child to create an entity containing elements from both parties, yet capable of remaining uniquely different.

7 – THE SCARLET WOMAN: NETZACH

All Goddesses of love and devotion, lust and desire correspond to Netzach. Here we find the Roman Venus, the Greek Aphrodite, Psyche, Artemis, and the Egyptian Nebthet and Hathoor. Netzach corresponds to the creative, emotional, devotional, artistic, and intuitive faculties. In this sephirah, we find feminine strength and sexuality.

8 – BAPHOMET: HOD

To me, Baphomet represents the potential of absorbing, reconciling, and using conflicting archetypes. It therefore nicely represents the intellectual attributions associated with Hod. No one seems to agree on the origin or meaning of this name; one of the meanings I find interesting is the connection to Binah one scholar makes by calling it "the baptism of the Mother."

According to Eliphas Levi, the image of Baphomet represents the union of opposites. The Devil Tarot card seems to indicate androgyny and bisexuality, and the power of the intellect responsible for the union of opposites, illustrating the state of the mind once the magician has transcended the first polarities on the Tree of Life.

9 – THERION: YESOD

Yesod is consistent with the archetypal idea of Therion. Travelers encounter the first polarity on the Tree of Life as they rise from Yesod toward Tiphareth and encounter Hod and Netzach. This progress is marked by the Tarot Trump Art, or Temperance, as it is called in some decks.

To progress, one must reconcile these principles, and the driving force behind that desire is appropriately congruent with Therion. The unconscious sexual drive to unite opposites is symbolized in Yesod. Therion, or "Beast" in the Greek language, seems to encompass that animal like quality expressed in the *Nephesh,* or animal consciousness.

10 – Ankh-Af-Na-Khonsu: Malkuth

In Malkuth, Ankh-Af-Na-Khonsu, the author of the Stelé of Reveal-ing, adores and performs his magick in accordance with the desire of his Beloved, in order to unite with his Goddess, Nuit.

The rub is that to unite with the Goddess, he must himself become a god. Not just any deity, but the counterpart of Nuit – Hadit. Every stage of his progress is plainly mapped out by the placement of the other gods on the sephiroth in the Middle Pillar.

Further Considerations on the Thelemic Gods

1. Dion Fortune states: "The First Path is called the Admirable or Hid-den Intelligence because it is the Light giving the power of com-prehension of the First Principle, which hath no beginning. And it is the Primal Glory, because no created being can attain to its essence" (Fortune 2000). This illustrates Kether's influence over Chokmah's appointment.

2. One of its many functions is mysteriously hinted at by one of its names. The Tower, Trump number 16, is understood by Adepts as ejaculation.

3. The Chalice is used to hold liquid. "The Mother," "The Sea," and "The Vagina" all allude to its many metaphorical and practical purposes.

1, 2, and 3. Metaphorically, Chokmah and Binah represent the two crucial substances (elemental in Alchemy, and chemical in Chemis-try) necessary to produce a third. Chokmah (the Phallus) contains the seed; Binah (the Yoni) contains the egg. What seed is used de-pends, perhaps, on Kether, and this is not so hard to swallow if we realize that (according to the *Sepher Yetzirah*) the Supernal Triangle (composed of Kether, Chokmah, and Binah) is but an illusion, and is in reality the one sephirah called Kether.

4, 5 and 6. Geburah (Ra-Hoor-Khuit) is Will. Chesed (Hoor-Par-Krat) is Love. These guard the Gates of the Abyss, and by their experience and the persistence of the magician, he is duly armed with a strong will and an unshakeable power of discrimination for his journey across the vast desert. The culmination of the three sephiroth on the Second Triad, or, as it is often called, "The Triad of Justice" or "Ruach," – Tiphareth, Chesed, and Geburah – compose the idea of Horus.

7. Netzach represents a feminine sexuality and strength, inconceivable and frightening to early Christianity (which is, after all, patriarchal); it is no wonder lust was denounced.

With the exception of Aleister Crowley, our Western predecessors (and even some of our contemporaries) perceive lust as a transgression, not recognizing its function or purpose in the human condition. It is one of the Catholic seven deadly sins, and has been misunderstood ever since the Church denounced it.

Dion Fortune, who lived in one of the most sexually oppressed times in history, classifies the vice of Netzach as lust and the virtue as unselfishness. When lust is recognized as the driving force of our desires and wants, we begin to appreciate what it is and how it works.

The lust for knowledge, for example, is responsible for our mental, spiritual, and physical growth. It is the driving force for everything we attempt, no matter how humble the motive may appear. It causes men and women alike to unite themselves with all things, wherever they are encountered in our attempt to discover greater truths. Without it we would be lost, as a race, in the evolutionary process.

We are initiated by sex – our lives, and ultimately our deaths, are the direct results of sexual union. The Scarlet Woman is the initiatress, and in her is all power given. The Eastern Tantric Masters refer to this archetypal woman as the "Dark Girl" who endows man with magical power and knowledge of sexual secrets. This is consistent with the idea that Netzach is a subtler, human form of Binah, the Dark Mother.

8. In Greek mythology, the result of the copulation between Hermes
   (Hod, Mercury) and Aphrodite (Netzach, Venus) was Hermaphroditus. Allegedly, the Aeon of Isis was matriarchal, and the Aeon of
   Osiris was patriarchal. It makes perfect sense that the present Aeon,
   the Aeon of The Child, would reconcile the differences of the previous two eras.

The Great Work

Without faith, Science leads to doubt; Without Science, faith leads to superstition. Uniting them brings certainty, but in so doing they must never be confused with each other. The object of faith is hypothesis, and this becomes certitude when the hypothesis is necessitated by evidence or by the demonstration of science. The acknowledgement of this link-up between the two basic elements of man's life results in tranquility of mind and peace of heart.

– Eliphas Levi

The Great Work consists of the sublime unity of Man and Spirit. In the mysteries, the pentagram symbolizes Man, and the Spirit of God is symbolized by the hexagram. The union of Man and Spirit could be symbolized by the 11-pointed star (5 + 6 = 11). Eleven is therefore the number of magick. This indicates that the aim of magick is union with God. In the Order of the Silver Star, the grade symbolizing this union is called 5=6 (Man embodies God), indicating that the marriage has been accomplished.

There is a Word that symbolizes this Union: ABRAHADABRA. It has 11 letters and contains five vowels, each of which is an A (the pentalpha, or pentagram, of five points). It also contains six consonants (the hexagram, six points). By the holy art of gematria, this word enumerates to 418. Careful study of this number will reveal several mysteries.

The Great Work means different things to different people, but on one level it is the method by which we become one with God. The methods by which we attain these heights are to be found in the Middle Pillar on the Tree of Life:

Malkuth =   Know Thyself
Yesod =   Discover your True Will
Tiphareth = Knowledge and Conversation with the Holy Guardian
             Angel
Kether =   Union with God

The Great Work is the path of return towards God. The task is not an easy one.

Self-discipline, or discipline of the mind, is the key in the beginning. Once you can quiet the mind and concentrate your thoughts on any given subject or object, the Work becomes almost second nature.

The next step is to discipline the body. You must learn to find specific positions in which your body can be both comfortable and rigid. This is referred to as asana.

Next, you must gain control over your breathing. As a rule, humans (with the exception of a few athletes) do not know how to breathe properly. The full potential of the lungs is not realized. This is important in the Work because oxygen is carried from the lungs into the blood stream, and is then carried to the brain to vitalize brain activity. In essence, one who knows how to breathe properly has a healthy mind. Too much oxygen is as unfavorable as not enough. The practice of breath control is called Pranayama.

The brain needs a specific amount of oxygen in order to operate properly. The Hindu alchemists discovered a responsive connection between breathing patterns and the amount of energy residing in the spinal column that they call Kundalini.

The Kundalini is understood as a current of raw energy that dwells at the base of the spine and is capable of springing straight up the spinal column to the third eye region. When this occurs, great magically related phenomena are believed to take place. Sex is said to stimulate this coiled serpent. The other method of stimulation is controlled breathing.

Breathing through the left nostril is said to stimulate a negative magnetic current called *Ida*. The properties of Ida are characteristic of Luna, but some believe it to be more congenial to Venus.

Breathing through the right nostril is understood to arouse a positive magnetic current called *Pingala*. The elements of Pingala are parallel to Sol, although some would argue that it is more closely related to Mars.

When one alternates breathing between one nostril and the other, these subtle energies ignite the coiled snake and entice it to rise up a hollow tube that runs the length of the spine; this is called *Sushumna*.

Therefore, the purpose of Pranayama or breath control is to awaken the latent energies inhabiting our bodies. For more on Pranayama, see the section on "Practical Exercises."

The Holy Guardian Angel vs. God

Be strong, o man! lust, enjoy all things of sense and rapture: fear not that any God shall deny thee for this.

— Liber Al II:22

Two people can look at a pencil and agree that it is a pencil, because the senses have sent their brains similar information. However, since two objects cannot occupy the same space at the same time, our perceptions will vary because our positions relative to the pencil will differ.

This illustrates the great fall of conventional religion. Every sect has a perspective of God that differs from other sects, and they will not allow any deviance from their perspective. They fail to realize that the experience of the knowledge of God is different to everyone, depending on where that person is in relation to the rest of the universe.

'God,' as a word, attempts to describe an entity that admittedly cannot be described, yet those who use this word while preaching will claim they know what God wants you to do. If God wants to tell you something, God will tell you personally.

According to the Scriptures, God wanted people to think independently, and for this reason, more and more Qabalists subscribe to the idea that it was God who disguised Himself as a Serpent to tempt Adam and Eve.

A Gnostic (one who *knows* God as opposed to one that has *faith* in the existence of God) must strive to develop to a personal relationship with God, without the middle man. Everything necessary to accomplish this is within our hearts; this is the mystery of the Christ. Conventional religious cults do not want you to know this. They want you to feel like you need them so they can continue selling real estate in heaven. Cults need to exercise control over their members; they are not in the least bit interested in their devotees developing a personal relationship with God.

Everyone should strive to create a personal religion according to individual Will and evolutionary development. It is a good idea to study all religions in order to understand the inner mysteries hidden therein. Only by this knowledge can you come to the understanding necessary to create your own myth. Religion has a lot to offer, and you can learn much about the cultures and lives of the people who follow the religion you are researching.

Remember – since Truth is beyond speech, it cannot be communicated. Therefore, to avoid folly when reading any holy book, you must not take the literal meaning as Truth or you will be in danger of falling into the same trap as the fundamentalist. Furthermore, don't trust anyone who claims to know the Truth. Truth is protected from the vulgar because it is written in a language that only the initiated will understand. Become worthy of the Truth and it will find you. The experience of God differs for each person because God manifests Itself to the individual according to individual circumstances, race, culture, education, and previous experience.

Because the Thelemic magician understands this basic principle of philosophy, Thelema uses the term Holy Guardian Angel when referring to a personal "God." The magician knows that the image in which God has manifested Itself to the individual is only one in an infinity at Its disposal.

Conventional philosophies go to great lengths to make people believe that their God is the only one. They boast about Its Omnipotence and Omnipresence, yet they fail to recognize the very same God as manifested in other cultures. In essence, they blaspheme the same God that they claim to serve.

The Holy Guardian Angel is your God. It will not make you drop to your knees, nor expect you to do the will of others. It will walk with you, be there in times of need to comfort you, and in times of great opposition It will be the blood that boils within you. It will laugh with you in times of great happiness and strengthen you in times of great sorrow.

The image that your angel has given you is uniquely yours. Remember to show others the benefit of knowing their own God, as the sages of time tell us, "In true religion there is no sect. Therefore take heed that thou blaspheme not the name by which another knoweth his God, for if thou doest this thing in Jupiter, thou wilt blaspheme YHVH, and in Osiris YEHESHUAH. Ask of God and ye shall have. Seek, and ye shall find. Knock, and it shall be opened unto you!" (*Liber Libræ Sub Figura XXX*)

PERCEPTION IS NINE TENTHS OF THE LAW

True Will vs. Destiny

Nothing resists the will of man, when he knows the truth, and wills the good.

– Eliphas Levi

The best way to explain the difference between True Will and destiny is to illustrate the way in which they affect our lives. The difference between them will reveal one of the many differences between Christianity and gnosis.

True Will is similar to what most people refer to as destiny, but there is one difference that goes far beyond the literary sense of both terms. Destiny implies a predetermined course that you must travel and an outcome over which you have no control. Your destiny is yours, like it or not. You are a pawn in a game called "life." You pray diligently to your God that you may be a worthy candidate for heaven, knowing all along (according to some schools of Christian thought) that God has already decided the outcome. To make matters worse, God won't even say what it is!

Destiny is also a convenient tool for blaming your problems on life, on the universe, and even on the God to which you pray. It's a way of getting even with God for being so silent.

True Will, on the other hand, implies *choice* and *purpose*. It is for those few who choose a more responsible approach in their roles as co-creators of the universe. These people do not plead nor beg for their God's acceptance; they are what their God has made them, and for that they make no apologies.

It could be said that True Will is destiny, transmuted into a form that allows you an active roll in your existence.

Once you find your True Will, you begin to see the deity that dwells within you. It then becomes unavoidable that you also recognize the deity dwelling in all other Stars. And there is a great consequence of this power – that which you wish upon some other, you also invoke upon yourself. Every word, deed, and thought must be pure in nature, so that it will lead you to the unity of all things.

Transmuting Destiny into True Will

The will of the just man is the Will of God himself, and the law of Nature.

— Eliphas Levi

As a magician, your first task is to find your destiny by studying the chain of events that have led you to your present physical, emotional, spiritual, and mental states. By reviewing specific events and spending considerable time meditating on them, you will eventually come to an understanding of yourself and where you are going. Thus you will discover your destiny. "Know thyself" has always been the foundation of our Work.

Write your life story, and review it often. It will have to be rewritten many times. This simple exercise will illustrate that every conclusion you come up with at any given time is an illusion that may be convenient, but is tentative at best.

The next step is to magically turn the tables around and get control of a seemingly uncontrollable force. Here the magician plays an unsurpassable game of "if you can't beat 'em, join 'em." He attaches himself to his destiny through an act of Love.

Once this has been successfully accomplished, the magician experiences a series of phenomena that change the concept of destiny into an understanding of True Will. You come to the realization that there is no other path you would rather travel. Because you are one with it, you can now play an active part in fulfilling it. You incarnated with the intention in the first place. Knowing your True Will or destiny amounts to becoming aware of what you came here to do – not what you were assigned to do by some external force. You are no longer a prisoner to the external forces that used to lead you by the nose. Instead, you are a key agent in your own creation. Because you are now going with the current of your original purpose, you have the inertia of the universe behind you. Destiny has been transmuted into True Will.

The Philosophy of True Will

To find the central clue to our moral being which unites us to the universal order, that indeed is the highest human attainment. For a long time people have seldom been capable of it.

                  – Confucius

As I have mentioned previously, doing your True Will means following the course that the universe has chosen for you and staying on it. Don't misunderstand – we have all been designed for a specific way (in the sense of "tao"). Staying on course is very easy once you know what your Will is, but perhaps the hardest part of all is refusing to allow anyone to interfere with *your* Will while remaining vigilant that you do not interfere with the Will of others.

"Every man and every woman is a star" (Crowley 2004). Everyone has a personal course that is unique to the individual. No matter how insignificant it may seem to you, your Will plays an important role within the divine plan. The Will doesn't always involve some earthshaking event. Some of us get to be doctors, musicians, lawyers, or Martin Luther King, while others get to be janitors, parents, or homeless. You have to embrace your Will no matter what it is, because it belongs to you.[1] Just as the stars in the heavens spend millennia traveling through the cosmos in perfect harmony, if one should veer off its course and collide with another, the whole universe would be affected. It is equally chaotic if we interfere with another person. Try to imagine a world where everyone followed his Will and encouraged fellow human beings to do the same!

Let's study the opening phrase of *Liber Al*; it's an important factor in this philosophy. No, more than that, it is our Law. "Do what thou wilt shall be the whole of the Law" (Crowley 2004). I have often greeted people with this sentence, and it has always been received cheerfully by everyone except those who know that their intentions, motivations, and desires are anything but pure. Let me remind you that this statement does not imply, "do what you want," because most of the things we desire only gratify the Ego and have no real value. Will may be

---

1 Let it be that state of manhood bound and loathing. So with thy all; thou hast no right but to do thy will. Do that, and no other shall say nay. For pure will, unassuaged of purpose, delivered from the lust of result, is every way perfect. – *Liber Al vel Legis: The Book of the Law*

related to, may be the same as, or may be the *complete opposite* of want.

The word "Thou" is taken from the Hebrew *ateh*, which was used by the ancients when addressing God. This sentence gives you, as a human being, the right to carry out your Will, presuming that you have united with it and are truly following the course chosen for you by your personal God. It is a lawful and noble task. One must constantly keep in mind the rules set forth above, and never interfere with the life of another in any way, shape, or form. I am referring to the divine Will, which is yours when you have unselfishly given yourself to it and to the service of mankind. As you may have noticed, "Love is the law, love under will" is the second half of the formula.

This philosophy has no beginning and no end. "Do what thou wilt" leads you to do as you love, but keeps it in check with your Will. We all do what we want, but what we want should be what we, in good conscience, Will. Of course, this has been simplified in order to illustrate some of its many implications.

This concept implies that love and Will are congruent, and that the only way to unite with Will is through love. Doing your Will is an act of love for humanity, the universe, and your God.

Who but a person in love would sacrifice so much of his life to aid and participate in the divine plan? Our goal is to evolve, to be more than human; but before we can start, we must possess a superhuman ability to love.

Ordeals

The more obstacles the will surmounts, the stronger it is. It is for this reason that Christ glorified poverty and sorrow.

– Eliphas Levi

When you stray from your course, you can expect to encounter opposition. This is not to say that if you have discovered your True Will, you will not suffer. After all, movement creates friction. Those of us who are going to live our lives on our own terms will have to be willing to take a few punches from time to time. All you have to do is read about the ailments associated with inactivity to agree that it is better to experience the ordeals life offers us than to restrict movement and growth. It doesn't take much imagination to speculate about the spiritual disorders caused by inertia.

The universe has many lessons to teach, and some come in the form of ordeals. Sometimes, knowing what is to occur is saddening enough, just as I'm sure it must have been for both Jesus and Judas in the Christian legend.

Balance is the basis of the Work of the macrocosm; as the microcosm, we must assist by keeping harmony within ourselves. We do this by following and staying on our Paths. When we stray, the scale tips and the universe has to compensate. This compensation, more often than not, manifests itself in an unpleasant form.

Karma and the ordeals I am referring to here are the same thing. When you have created an imbalance, the universe will present you with the situation best suited to correct this imbalance as quickly and effectively as possible.

No matter how painful the ordeal may be, it must be treated as an adventure. Keep in mind that, up until this point, every ordeal's purpose has been to prepare you for the kind of life you are now living. See where current circumstances are leading you, and how they are changing your life, and use this information to find out where you are going. It is an honor to know that you have been worthy of instruction. Remember that you placed yourself where you are now. Remember that ancient dictum, the oath of the Magister Templi: "I will interpret every phenomenon as a particular dealing of God with my Soul."

Knowledge

The decisive question for man is: Is he related to the infinite or not?
That is the telling question of his life. Only if we know that the thing
which truly matters is the infinite can we avoid fixing our interests
upon futilities and upon all kinds of goals which are not of real
importance.

– Carl Jung

Knowledge, as applied to magick, is very different from conventional knowledge. In a rapidly expanding scientific age where computers are a common as automobiles, the word "knowledge" has come to mean "having information." It is quite different when it comes to the magical art.

Today's magician behaves as though someone has unscrewed the top of his head and vomited Regardie's *Golden Dawn* and Crowley's *Magick in Theory and Practice* into it. Rather than using the superb instruction offered by such books to gain mastery over ritual, the student repeats what is read but is unable to contribute anything new. Knowledge, to a real magician, is experience.

I have said elsewhere that one cannot *know* what an apple tastes like from another's efforts to describe it. The advantage of having knowledge of a particular subject is that the response from a particular action is somewhat predictable.

A dabbler may have a lot of information about magick and talk a great deal about make-believe successes, but only the magician will have enough knowledge to determine the outcome of any specific ritual. Like children, we learn by doing.

Knowledge outlasts time, but information is constantly being replaced by updated information; it has no endurance. Strive, therefore, to experience all things rather than just to collect information. Gathering information is for those who, because of their fear of death, experience life through the eyes of brave men.

Courage

Courage means being afraid and saddling up anyway.
                                        – John Wayne

Perhaps the biggest pitfall for magicians is fear. Fear manifests where there is a lack of knowledge. A lack of understanding can create a feeling of fear towards a subject, idea, or object. This is because, in each case, the mind tries to anticipate the future of a situation based on previous experience of similar situations, calling up all information related to the experience(s). If there is insufficient information, a fear of the unknown manifests. This fear can interfere with your efforts, making you feel incompetent and persuading you to abandon the Work.

The most dangerous fear is created by things that are *half understood*. When your mind searches for data associated with the experience, it pieces together preconceptions out of the little and incomplete information you may retain in conscious memory.

While the following illustration may be somewhat crude, it serves to make a point: A child touches a stove and is burned. If he is not taught that stoves aren't always hot or instructed in the proper behavior around hot appliances, it's possible that the child will have a distorted image of stoves for the rest of his life. The fear created by the *child*'s experience and assumptions will prevent the *adult* from discovering a sane method of utilizing these appliances.

Fear is a built in safety device that keeps us from repeating mistakes. But when it dominates what we think and do, when our actions are based on misconception, then fear has become our master. This is why it is so important to finish the Work you have started. If you leave anything half finished, it will only be half understood, leaving the phantasm in your mind with the grim chore of finishing it for you…in any way it can.

Love

Love is a God; Strong, free, unabounded, and as some define Fears nothing, pitieth none.

– Milton

Love is one of the trickiest things to talk about, because the word has had so many untruths pumped into it.

The underlying essence of real Love (Agape) is unconditional. You cannot Love one thing and hate another. The delusion that you can separate yourself from any other thing is created by Ego, which uses lust of result, bigotry, or a false pride as its weapons. Common or profane love usually hurts or wounds, and when we feel the prick of its thorn, many of us learn to shut ourselves off to authentic Love. Our hearts harden like tempered steel. Every time we confuse profane love with sacred Love, we become a little more calloused and resistant. This may happen to such an extreme that when Love comes our way, it is confused with the lesser love and is not allowed to find its true place within our hearts. A very perceptive man once said that the only kind of falling that is not failing is falling in Love.

The kind of Love referred to in conjunction with magick is unknown to most people. When our lives are being lived to their fullest potential and all the little ordeals that come our way when we stray from our path have disappeared, that's when we are likely to experience Love.

It manifests as golden light. Everything you look at suddenly has a golden aura around it. There is a feeling of excitement and rediscovery. The things you took for granted have suddenly changed. They must be re-experienced under this new Light. You are likely to experience newfound trust and hope in people, because you are able to recognize the deity within them. Everything is possible now. You have become as a child.

Love is unity. Meditation is impossible without it. Every time we attempt to fully experience another object, we must unite with it. Without the ability to Love, we cannot do this. When dealing with other people, this could, and usually does, manifest in sex.

Sex can be the highest sacrament, but it must be brought from a *nephesh* (animal consciousness) level to a level of *nashama* (highest aspirations of the soul). This is only possible if the act is being motivated by the unifying factor of Love.

Being able to unite with object and subject is only a small step into the countless possibilities of the experiences dealing with Love. When you have mastered Love, you will have completely united with it, so that it burns and communicates to others through you. You will then have harnessed that mysterious energy that turns lead into gold.

In those scarce moments when two people feel pure, unadulterated Love for each other, an astral bond is created. Psychic phenomena may be experienced often, as an inner rapport is created between individuals. "Love is the law, love under will" – one of the many mysteries of this law is to love all creation. By so doing, the magician will develop an astral connection with the whole of the cosmos.

All in all, Love is a rare commodity in this world. It doesn't come often. When it does, you should be prepared to recognize it. If you are fortunate enough to find someone to love, consider what a privilege it is that this person(s) has found you worthy of sharing their universe. Respect them; recognize their right to be themselves, to be free-thinking individuals, and then embrace them as loosely as you can.

Silence

Let us be silent, that we may hear the whispers of the gods.
— Emerson

Of the four magical powers, Silence is perhaps the most important. It can prevent painful situations in your life. The previous aeon has left a dangerous poison in the group mind of western civilization. You have only to look at history to realize that everything of value the holy books had to offer was altered by those in authority, to make slaves of the simple man.

The Church has been in power so long, and the Scriptures inaccurate for so many generations that even its leaders are in the dark as to the true meanings of their manual.

Conventional religions preach that all one must do is believe. You are not to question the Scriptures. This is done to prevent free thinking and as a result, the masses have become gullible, lazy, and easily controlled by those in power. To find truth in anything, one must have a thirst for knowledge; one must question all things. It takes a lot of hard work. Western religion, with its dogma, has created a breed of humans who do not question the motives of those in authority and are too lazy to seek the truth for themselves. They believe anything their superiors tell them, because their superiors appear to have done the work *they* have avoided. What does this have to do with Silence?

Study the history of the Church and you will see that many innocent people have been tortured and killed, simply because they would not submit their will to the Church. How many cultures has it completely erased by making so-called "good Christians" out of so-called "savages"? How many battles have been fought in the name of the Church, with good people lost on both sides just to satisfy the lust for power and money? It has even prosecuted its own people for questioning its motives.

By keeping your Work secret, it is magically charged and sanctified. When ancient Egyptian adepts inherited the name of a spirit or god, they zealously kept it from the profane, for by uttering the name, the named forces were summoned.

Besides consecrating your Work, Silence reduces the chances of those unsympathetic to magick interfering with your operations. Do not allow doubt to enter into your Work if you have allowed others to interfere. Test all things, and hold fast to what is good. Enough said about ignorance.

There are other reasons why Silence is so important to magical Work. We all know people who talk a great deal and do nothing. It would appear that talking about magick brings them more satisfaction than actually doing it. You can talk right through your enthusiasm for a project, so that when it comes down to actually grounding it, you have none left.

To explain this further, we have to study how thought is filtered from the archetypal plane to the material plane. All truly great ideas believed to be inspired by genius are in fact sparks of the divine. One adept at channeling such ideas has mastered the methods of tuning in to that plane.

These sparks come from the archetypal plane. The archetypes, being abstract by nature, are beyond intellectual understanding. The spark must go through a process of solidification and materialization, just as a fertilized egg does before being transformed into a fetus.

The spark descends downwards to the creative plane. This is the womb, where all great thoughts are conceived. There it stays for a while, until it is transformed into a symbol.

Once the creative plane has matured this symbol, it flows down to the formative plane. When it has reached this step, and not before, you begin to realize that something is going on in your mind, demanding attention. Although it may still be rough, the idea is realized. It must be shaped and prepared so that it can descend even further and manifest in material form on the physical plane.

The problems begin as you become aware of the activity in your mind. It is easy to gratify your sense of ego by boasting of your still unmanifest project, until the continuity between the higher and lower planes is disrupted. The link becomes weak, and the concept is aborted. Silence is very important indeed in magical Work.

To further illustrate the significance of Silence, I include this bit of information: Research by marriage counselors shows that couples who only thought of the carnal aspects of lovemaking had no problem talking about it with others. Couples who respected their partners and thought of their lovemaking as special would not talk about it with their counselors. They had made their lovemaking sacred.

We show this kind of devotion with our Work. Don't kiss and tell, and do not throw your pearls before swine.

Life

Beauty and strength, leaping laughter and delicious languor, force and fire, are of us.

— Liber AL II:20

Opportunity – the atheist looks for it, the mystic waits for it, and the magician creates it. It's easy to waste an incarnation looking and waiting. *Doing* and *going* are the functions of a god. There are many armchair magicians who flatter themselves by amazing their friends, talking about magick and about how efficient they have become in a particular rite. But they forget the most important tool in successful ritual: the Magical Link. All the power that ever was, is, and will be, is here now. Ritual is action. It is used to cause change in conformity with Will. Part of the ritual has to involve physical movement, an involvement in the particular area that you are trying to change.

For example, you might feel the need to do a ritual to prevent the environmental disaster that lies ahead. You can do ritual until you are blue in the face; however, unless you protest the dumping of toxic waste into the ocean, the spraying of pesticides on our food, or the deforestation of the Amazon, there is little chance that you will have an effect. You are the Magical Link. The Magical Link is the conduit connecting the higher forces that magick stimulates with the goal you are trying to effect.

What does this have to do with life? Everything! If you assume that magick is the art of living, then properly done ritual is the key to a successful life. Every step of your everyday life should include deliberate acts of worship.

You are the creator of your universe; you mold it, shape it, and become it. If you stand idle, chances are others will shape it for you.

Live the moment now; it is the only thing that exists. The past is no longer here, and while it may have altered your evolutionary status, it is gone. The future is not here yet, so waiting for it to happen will only make you waste the precious now.

Live every moment like it is your last. Embrace life now! Experience all that is going on around you, and enjoy it as a sacrament unto the Goddess, for She is experience.

There are many people unhappy with their lives who don't realize they hold the key to a better life in their hands! Shakespeare once said, "All the world's a stage." If you don't like the part you are play-ing, change scripts!

The successful magician easily adapts to his environment. It is not to be conquered! You must become one with it so that you are an active player in its fulfillment, responding to situations rather than reacting.

Death

Think not, o king, upon that lie: That Thou Must Die: verily thou shalt not die, but live.

– Liber AL II:21

As if it wasn't enough to justify one's own existence, man has also tried to discover what lies ahead after the physical body ceases to cooperate in this thing we call "life."

The deity within us all constantly plays hide and seek. And as jolly good sports, we play the endless game knowing that we will probably not find it. After all, it's not the kill, but the thrill of the chase. We are all hunters.

Maybe our fascination with the afterlife comes from the subconscious knowledge that we are as gods. Maybe it is one of the necessary steps in self-discovery... a lot of maybes.

We have heard countless stories from people who have died and, for one reason or another, have returned. While not all of them remembered what it was like being clinically dead, most who *did* remember experienced a similar vision: the vision of the white light.

We know that light is a wave which changes color according to the speed of its vibration. The Tree of Life is a glyph containing ten colored spheres (which have been called "The ten faces of God") and the 22 paths that connect them. Look at the uppermost sphere that we know as Kether and let's call that "Light," fluid, moving, etc. The whole of the universe is concentrated and focused within one miniscule dot.

Now let's look at the bottom sphere: Malkuth, the Kingdom, the material plane, the place where all souls experience life in human bodies. Let's call that "Physical existence."

The pure Light emanating from Kether slows down as it moves away from its nucleus, changing color and gaining density as it moves away from its source. The other spheres on the Tree display the different stages of this transmutation.

The ancients have told us, "Kether is in Malkuth, and Malkuth is in Kether, but after another manner," or "As above, so below." They were trying to point out that as Kether was Malkuth, Light was Darkness, Fluidness was Solid, etc., after each had been transformed by a separation within itself – a division, much like that of a cell.

Malkuth is solidified Light. We are that Light made solid. *The Book of the Law* says: "For I am divided for love's sake, for the chance of union." The Great Work is the Path of Return, the return to the source. This holy book also says: "There is no bond that can unite the divided but love." This tells us that the driving force of the journey back is Love. The journey ends when we reach that Light from whence we came: Kether, union with the Goddess. We are intended to accomplish this union consciously.

Death is the friend of the weary traveler who has lost his way; it is the initiating officer to the mysteries of immortality. It is not to be feared, but welcomed as an ally and respected as a teacher that will one day provide you with the opportunity to look at Our Lady of the Stars, face to face.

Why Thelema?

The old gods are dead or dying and people everywhere are searching, asking: What is the new mythology to be?

— Joseph Campbell

As you read this book, you may be asking yourself, "why would anyone want to attune to a new form of thought while there are already very powerful, well organized religions with the benefit of thousands of years of trial and error?"

The answer is quite simple: there is a phenomenon that occurs in the universe every 2,000 to 5,000 years called the Equinox of the Gods. At this time, there is a change in the universal unconsciousness that dominates the evolutionary process of humans. The different shifts are represented by gods (usually Egyptian) whose virtues will demonstrate the fate of the next reign. There have been (so far as we have archaeological data) three such shifts in the evolution of humanity.

The Aeon of Isis. This period was matriarchal. Women were worshiped as gods for their ability to bear, nurture, and care for their young. Queens ruled the tribes, and the women were viewed as the strong ones. There are indications that women did the hunting and fought battles alongside of men. It was a time of respect for nature, as people loved Her and lived in harmony with Her.

The Aeon of Osiris. Osiris ruled the next Aeon. His jealous brother Set cut him into pieces and threw him into the Nile. Osiris's wife Isis, stricken with grief, gathered his body parts and used the magick of Thoth (Lord of Magick) to resurrect him. It was the era of the sacrificial gods, marking the beginning of Judaism and Christianity. This change occurred when man realized that he had a role in conception – primarily insemination. Suddenly, women were treated as second rate citizens, weaker, and less intelligent than men. Man ceased to live in harmony with Nature, choosing instead to have dominion over Her. Mankind was to serve the male god as slaves. The last traces of this oppressive era are still with us today. We can see its influence on the environment and in places where women and minorities are oppressed.

The Aeon of Horus. In 1904, another such shift occurred. The angel Aiwass dictated the threefold *Book of the Law* and proclaimed that Horus, the hawk-headed God, had taken his place on the Throne of

the Gods. The Victorian-age magician Aleister Crowley was the conduit. This era marks the Aeon of the Child, the word of whose Law is
Thelema. The Law encompasses all true religions and is capable of
great tolerance, essential to protect the diversity it conveys. Here, we
are facing the liberation of the entire human race from those who
have oppressed it.

Horus is the Egyptian God of war, and recently we have seen him
do his thing in Germany (at the Berlin Wall), Yugoslavia, Poland, the
Soviet Union, South Korea, and Tiananmen Square in China. The
masses cry for freedom.

The Aeon of Osiris has had a very strong influence in the last 2,000
years. Even those who do not subscribe to its dogma are influenced
by it in one way or another. Most codes of morality are based on its
principles. This current has dominated for so long that we are presented with the opportunity to reflect on it and see how its poison has
affected the world.

It portrays women as troublemakers who cannot keep secrets, as
weaker and less intelligent than men, untrustworthy. It has even gone
so far as to explain the pain of childbirth and menstrual bleeding as
punishments from God for having deceived man. Women in this day
are still fighting for the equality they deserve.

It has led man to believe that Nature cannot exist without him. All
we have to do is watch TV or read a newspaper to realize our impact
on the environment. It is inconceivable that, after millions of years
of evolution, there are people who still believe Nature is to be dominated. We are told that God doesn't live here, and we are discouraged
from showing affection or allegiance to the Earth. We can already see
what this kind of thinking has done to the condition of our Mother.

The Church will not condone the use of condoms. It believes that
people should abstain from sex. As a result, the rate of unwanted preg-
nancy is increasing at an alarming rate, not to mention the sexually
transmitted diseases that are destroying so many lives. It is curious to
see that the same people who oppose birth control also oppose abortion, sex education, and Planned Parenthood. Abortion would cease
to exist if religious zealots understood the true effects of sex education and did not obstruct birth control technology. When it comes to
human sexuality, we are still living in the Dark Ages.

During the Inquisition, thousands of innocent people were tortured and killed in the name of God. Many of these were midwives

taking business away from the growing (and primarily male) medical profession. Things have not changed much since those days. Some U.S. states want to jail midwives for their services to couples who have lost their faith in the scientific age. Most decisions that our political leaders make conform with old Aeon ideas, with very little regard to common sense and intelligence, and even less consideration to the rights of the individual.

The burning and censoring of books and art still occurs today. Others control what we watch, see, eat, and listen to.

We are taught that any deviance from conventional religion is Satanic, evil, etc. On August 15, 1989, the fundamentalist movement declared on national television that the Star of David, the pentagram, and even the peace sign are signs of the devil – the hexagram, a geometric representation of God; the pentagram, a geometric representation of Man; and the peace sign, a symbol of utopian society.

It is easy to see the impact this kind of thinking has had on our global evolutionary development: brother has turned against brother for the sake of tradition, as in the case of the Catholic Priest Miguel Molinos. This devoted priest was sentenced to life in prison because he published a book in which he taught that 'inward prayer' (meditation) was more effective than outward prayer. This information, if embraced by the majority, would have made confession via a priest obsolete. The fact that he was one of the most devout members of the Church at the time of his arrest had little influence on the power-hungry individuals who condemned him. The book is *The Spiritual Guide of Miguel Molinos*. I strongly recommend it as a guide to developing a *personal* relationship with God.

Fundamentalism spends millions of dollars every year printing material to encourage new membership, while there are homeless men, women, and children who could be helped by these same dollars. It is obvious that the Church's emphasis is on membership rather than service.

For the last 2,000 years, we have been told that sex is filthy, that lovemaking is only for the purposes of procreation. This mentality is responsible for a great percentage of violent sexual crime, child abuse, sexual dysfunction, psychosis, etc. The beauty and selflessness of giving oneself to another has been turned into a hideous crime against God.

We are told not to question the Scriptures. Man has become lazy and gullible as a result. We don't question anything, and we believe whatever we are told. We are expected to refrain from interpreting the Scriptures, because they fear that we might find truth therein. To guard against this, the Scriptures have been altered so much that no one knows the truth anymore. This manipulation has affected the way we view life in general. We do not question what our politicians do, what they spray in our food, what they put into the ground, etc. And when we do ask, we believe everything they tell us. Thelema demands that we think for ourselves.

A newborn child is the most innocent and pure of all things. Yet children are baptized by parents who have been forced to believe their child is unclean, born through sin. This insult shows to what degree the Church influences the things we do and the reasons we do them.

Religious zealots have created a group mind that welcomes the destruction of the planet. It is held to be a fact that before the savior comes back, the world must first face a terrible ordeal. *The Book of Revelation* clearly marks the end of the Osirian Aeon, but seen through the eyes of the vulgar, it is the end of the world. The group mind has greatly affected the condition of the planet.

We have a duty to return to Nature what belongs to Her. There was a time when it took years to travel from one part of the country to another. We can now do it in a matter of hours; we have reduced the world to a speck of dust. Yet with all of this technology, there are still people dying of hunger all over the world. Wars are waged to keep something or to take something from someone else. When religion stands in the way of evolution or the creation of utopia, it is time for a *new* religion.

These old ideas cannot help us to further our evolutionary objective; they are full of hate and bigotry, and can do nothing more than hold back the human race. The world needs an alternative – true freedom. The world needs the freedom to fulfill its best potential without the interference of a twisted, demented creed designed specifically to control people. Nature needs respect from Man. We must learn to work with Her, not against Her, and then perhaps we can stop the destruction of the planet.

With all that's been said above, it is hard to understand why anyone would bother with religion in the first place. Quite simply, Man is made up of physical, mental, and spiritual matter. To deny these aspects a means of expression would cause an involuntary imbalance in our natural makeup. Religion and myth are the tools the Beloved uses to create the beings we have chosen to become, just as the potter uses the wheel and the kiln to create something that once existed only in the imagination of the creator.

Thelema offers the solution to the imbalance created by an oppressive society. As humans, it is our duty to evolve, to carry the vision of future generations on our shoulders. This is the Great Work. One day the Aeon of Horus will pass, and Thelema will no longer be the Word of the Law. A new order will rule for an Aeon. There will be other battles and principles, and it is my guess that we will be here once again to fight them.

The following thesis is based on the code of conduct of those who accept the Law of Thelema.

Duty by Aleister Crowley

(A note on the chief rules of practical conduct to be observed by those who accept the Law of Thelema.)

Do what thou wilt shall be the whole of the Law.
There is no law beyond Do what thou wilt.
...thou hast no right but to do thy will. Do that and no other shall say nay. For pure will, unassuaged of purpose, delivered from the lust of result, is every way perfect. 'Love is the law, love under will.
Every man and every woman is a star.

A. YOUR DUTY TO YOURSELF

1. *Find yourself to be the centre of your own Universe* "I am the flame that burns in every heart of man, and in the core of every star."

2. *Explore the Nature and Powers of your own Being.*
This includes everything which is, or can be for you: and you must accept everything exactly as it is in itself, as one of the factors which go to make up your True Self. This True Self thus ultimately includes all things soever: its discovery is Initiation (the traveling inwards) and as its Nature is to move continually, it must be understood not as static, but as dynamic, not as a Noun but as a Verb.

3. *Develop in due harmony and proportion every faculty which you possess.*
"Wisdom says: be strong!"
"But exceed! exceed!"
"Be strong, o man, lust, enjoy all things of sense and rapture: fear not that any God shall deny thee for this."

4. *Contemplate your own Nature.*
Consider every element thereof both separately and in relation to all the rest as to judge accurately the true purpose of the totality of your Being.

5. *Find the formula of this purpose, or "True Will" in an expression as simple as possible.*
Leave to understand clearly how best to manipulate the energies

which you control to obtain the results most favourable to it from its relations with the part of the Universe which you do not yet control.

6. *Extend the dominion of your consciousness, and its control of all forces alien to it, to the utmost.*

Do this by the ever stronger and more skilful application of your faculties to the finer, clearer, fuller, and more accurate perception, the better understanding, and the more wisely ordered government, of that external Universe.

7. *Never permit the thought or will of any other Being to interfere with your own.*

Be constantly vigilant to resent, and on the alert to resist, with unvanquishable ardour and vehemence of passion unquenchable, every attempt of any other Being to influence you otherwise than by contributing new facts to your experience of the Universe, or by assisting you to reach a higher synthesis of Truth by the mode of passionate fusion.

8. *Do not repress or restrict any true instinct of your Nature; but devote all in perfection to the sole service of your one True Will.*

"Be goodly therefore"

"The Word of Sin is Restriction. O man! refuse not thy wife if she will. O lover, if thou wilt, depart. There is no bond that can unite the divided but love: all else is a curse. Accursed! Accursed! be it to the aeons. Hell. So with thy all: thou hast no right but to do thy will. Do that and no other shall say nay. For pure will, unassuaged of purpose, delivered from the lust of result, is every way perfect."

"Ye shall gather goods and store of women and Spices; ye shall exceed the nations of the earth is Splendour & pride; but always in the love of me, and so shall ye come to my joy."

9. *Rejoice!*

"Remember all ye that existence is pure joy; that all the sorrows are but shadows; they pass & are done; but there is that which remains."

"But ye, o my people, rise up and awake! Let the rituals be rightly performed with joy and beauty!...A feast for fire and a feast for water; a feast for life and a greater feast for death! A feast every day in your hearts in the joy of my rapture. A feast every night unto Nuit, and the pleasure of uttermost delight. Aye! feast! rejoice! there is no dread hereafter. There is no dissolution and eternal ecstacy in the kisses of Nu."

"Now rejoice! now come in our splendour and rapture! Come in our passionate peace, & write sweet words for the Kings!"

"Thrill with the joy of life & death! Ah! thy death shall be lovely: whose seeth it shall be glad. Thy death shall be the seal of the promise of our agelong love. Come! lift up thy heart & rejoice!"

"Is God to live in a dog? No! but the highest are of us. They shall rejoice: who sorroweth is not of use. Beauty and strength, leaping laughter and delicious langour, force and fire, are of us."

B. Your Duty To Other Individual Men And Women

1. *"Love is the law, love under will."*
Unite yourself passionately with every other form of consciousness, thus destroying the sense of separateness from the Whole, and creating a new base-line in the Universe from which to measure it.

2. *"As brothers fight ye."*
"If he be a king thou canst not hurt him." To bring out saliently the differences between two points-of-view is useful to both in measuring the position of each in the whole. Combat stimulates the virile or creative energy; and, like love, of which it is one form, excites the mind to an orgasm which enables it to transcend its rational dullness.

3. *Abstain from all interferences with other wills.*
"Beware lest any force another King against King!" (The love and war in the previous injunctions are of the nature of sport, where one respects, and learns from the opponent, but never interferes with him, outside the actual game.) To seek to dominate or influence another is to seek to deform or destroy him; and he is a necessary part of one's own Universe, that is, of one's self.

4. *Seek, if you so will, to enlighten another when need arises.*
This may be done, always with the strict respect for the attitude of the good sportsman, when he is in distress through failure to understand himself clearly, especially when he specifically demands help; for his darkness may hinder one's perception of his perfection. (Yet

also his darkness may serve as a warning, or excite one's interest.) It is also lawful when his ignorance has lead him to interfere with one's will. All interference is in any case dangerous, and demands the exercise of extreme skill and good judgement, fortified by experience. To influence another is to leave one's citadel unguarded; and the attempt commonly ends in losing one's own self-supremacy.

5. *Worship all!*
   "Every man and every woman is a star."
   "Mercy let be off: damn those who pity."
   "We have nothing with the outcast and the unfit: let them die in their misery: For they feel not. Compassion is the vice of kings: stamp down the wretched and the weak: this is the law of the strong: this is our law and the joy of the world. Think not, o king, upon that lie: That Thou Must Die: verily thou shalt not die, but live! Now let it be understood if the body of the King dissolve, he shall remain in pure ecstacy for ever. Nuit Hadit Ra-Hoor-Khuit. The Sun, Strength and Sight, Light these are for the servants of the Star & the Snake."

   Each being is, exactly as you are, the sole centre of a Universe in no wise identical with, or even assimilable to, your own. The impersonal Universe of "Nature" is only an abstraction, approximately true, of the factors which it is convenient to regard as common to all. The Universe of another is therefore necessarily unknown to, and unknowable by, you; but it induces currents of energy in yours by determining in part your reactions. Use men and women, therefore, with the absolute respect due to inviolable standards of measurement; verify your own observations by comparison with similar judgements made by them; and, studying the methods which determine their failure or success, acquire for yourself the wit and skill required to cope with your own problems.

C. Your Duty To Mankind

1. *Establish the Law of Thelema as the sole basis of conduct.*
   The general welfare of the race being necessary in many respects to your own, that well-being, like your own, principally a function of the intelligent and wise observance of the Law of Thelema, it is of the very first importance to you that every individual should accept frankly that Law, and strictly govern himself in full accordance therewith.

You may regard the establishment of the Law of Thelema as an essential element of your True Will, since, whatever the ultimate nature of that Will, the evident condition of putting it into execution is freedom from external interference.

Governments often exhibit the most deplorable stupidity, however enlightened may be the men who compose and constitute them, or the people whose destinies they direct. It is therefore incumbent on every man and woman to take the proper steps to cause the revisions of all existing statutes on the basis of the Law of Thelema. This Law being a Law of Liberty, the aim of the legislation must be to secure the amplest freedom for each individual in the state, eschewing the presumptuous assumption that any given positive ideal is worthy to be obtained. "The Word of Sin is Restriction."

The essence of crime is that it restricts the freedom of the individual outraged. (Thus, murder restricts his right to live; robbery, his right to enjoy the fruits of his labour; coining, his right to the guarantee of the State that he shall barter in security; etc.) It is then the common duty to prevent crime by segregating the criminal, and by the threat of reprisals; also, to teach the criminal that his acts, being analyzed, are contrary to his own True Will. (This may often be accomplished by taking from him the right which he has denied to others; as by outlawing the thief, so that he feels constant anxiety for the safety of his own possessions, removed from the ward of the State.) The rule is quite simple. He who violated any right declares magically that it does not exist; therefore it no longer does so, for him.

Crime being a direct spiritual violation of the Law of Thelema, it should not be tolerated in the community. Those who possess the instinct should be segregated in a settlement to build up a state of their own, so to learn the necessity of themselves imposing and maintaining rules of justice.

All artificial crimes should be abolished. When fantastic restrictions disappear, the greater freedom of the individual will itself teach him to avoid acts which really restrict natural rights. Thus real crime will diminish dramatically.

The administration of the Law should be simplified by training men of uprightness and discretion whose will is to fulfill this function in the community to decide all complaints by the abstract principle of the Law of Thelema, and to award judgement on the basis of the actual restriction caused by the offense.

The ultimate aim is thus to reintegrate conscience, on true scientific principles, as the warden of conduct, the monitor of the people, and the guarantee of the governors.

D. Your Duty To All Other Beings And Things

1. *Apply the Law of Thelema to all problems of fitness, use, and development.*

It is a violation of the Law of Thelema to abuse the natural qualities of any animal or object by diverting it from its proper function, as determined by consideration of its history and structure. Thus, to train children to perform mental operations, or to practice tasks, for which they are unfitted, is a crime against nature. Similarly, to build houses of rotten material, to adulterate food, to destroy forests, etc., etc., is to offend.

The Law of Thelema is to be applied unflinchingly to decide every question of conduct. The inherent fitness of any thing for any proposed use should be the sole criterion.

Apparent, and sometimes even real, conflict between interests will frequently arise. Such cases are to be decided by the general value of the contending parties in the scale of Nature. Thus, a tree has a right to its life; but a man being more than a tree, he may cut it down for fuel or shelter when need arises. Even so, let him remember that the Law never fails to avenge infractions: as when wanton deforestation has ruined a climate or a soil, or as when the importation of rabbits for a cheap supply of food has created a plague.

Observe that the violation of the Law of Thelema produces cumulative ills. The drain of the agricultural population to big cities, due chiefly to persuading them to abandon their natural ideals, has not only made the country less tolerable to the peasant, but debauched the town. And the error tends to increase in geometrical progression, until a remedy has become almost inconceivable and the whole structure of society is threatened with ruin.

The wise application based on observation and experience of the Law of Thelema is to work in conscious harmony with Evolution. Experiments in creation, involving variation from existing types, are lawful and necessary. Their value is to be judged by their fertility as bearing witness to their harmony with the course of nature towards perfection.

A Better Society

Monarchy is based on the premise that one man is wiser than one million men. Democracy is based on the premise that a million men are wiser than one man. Both ideas are absurd.

— Robert Heinlein

The following is a manuscript written by Aleister Crowley describing the nature of the most elemental rights of every individual. It must be remembered that it was written at a time when the English language was male dominated. Since I am not the author of this piece, I am obligated to present it in its original form.

LIBER LXXVII, or LIBER OZ:

"the law of the strong: this is our law and the joy of the world." –AL. II. 2
"Do what thou wilt shall be the whole of the Law." –AL. I. 40
"thou hast no right but to do thy will. Do that, and no other shall say nay."
–AL. I. 42-3
"Every man and every woman is a star." –AL. I. 3
There is no god but man.

1. Man has the right to live by his own law—
   to live in the way that he wills to do:
   to work as he will:
   to play as he will:
   to rest as he will:
   to die when and how he will.
2. Man has the right to eat what he will:
   to drink what he will: to dwell where he will:
   to move as he will on the face of the earth.
3. Man has the right to think what he will:
   to speak what he will: to write what he will:
   to draw, paint, carve, etch, mould, build as he will:
   to dress as he will.
4. Man has the right to love as he will:–
   "take your fill and will of love as ye will,
   when, where, and with whom ye will." –AL. I. 51
5. Man has the right to kill those who would thwart these rights.
   "the slaves shall serve." –AL. II. 58
   "Love is the law, love under will." –AL. I. 57

Diet

"He who has health has hope, he who has hope has everything."
– Arabian Proverb

The magician is like a battery, with the capacity to store and manipulate energy and current. Pranayama and exercise affect our capacity to hold energy. Through physical movement, we become more efficient vehicles to carry this Life Force with us. Diet affects the energy and current. It would be of little value to become perfect vessels, only to fill ourselves with dead matter or low energy substances.

In today's world, we are faced with a unique problem. Science can keep us alive longer than ever before, but the quality of living has gone downhill. Our environment is so bad that we have to depend on those methods of life extension, because living in this filthy, polluted world is killing us. Even the food we eat can harm us due to the processing it requires before it gets to our tables, processes which strip nutritional value and add artificial ingredients in its place. Pesticides are sprayed on our fruits and vegetables, and waxes are added to make them appear to be fresh.

The animals we eat are fed antibiotics that we absorb when eating the meat, which is dyed to a bright red to appear more appetizing. Our bodies adjust to the accumulative levels of antibiotics until they become worthless to us in treating infection. Because the cattle rancher mixes these antibiotics indiscriminately with the cattle's food, the body of the animal ultimately becomes the perfect breeding ground for medicine-tolerant bacteria. This bacteria is absorbed into our bodies when we consume the flesh of the animal, and because we have developed a tolerance to antibiotics, we are not able to treat the resultant ailment.

Farmers continually add chemicals to the soil, which are then absorbed by the vegetation we eat. These same chemicals eventually make their way into the water we drink.

Processing hurts all food. When wheat is 'refined,' it loses over 20 nutrients in the process. The flour manufacturer returns four or five chemical nutrients to it and then calls it 'enriched.' Wheat and bread are subjected to roughly 80 chemicals in the growing and manufacturing process. Some of these chemicals stay in the finished product, to be eaten by the unsuspecting consumer.

There is a substance in all living things called Prana. Prana is the life force within; it is responsible for the vitality of all living organisms. All vegetables, fruits, and animals have Prana; the condition, biological makeup, and size of the item determines the amount of Prana it contains. Prana comes from nutrients in the soil or food that plants and animals consume. Without it, all living things would die.

Human beings require Prana for our survival. We acquire it from the foods we consume, the sun we are exposed to, and the air we breathe. It makes sense to consume only those foods with the highest amount of Prana in them. Prana will stay within fruits, vegetables, and meats after they have been picked or slaughtered, for varying times determined by the condition they were in at their life's termination.

Problematically, humans have longer intestinal tracts and weaker digestive acids than most meat-eating animals. This creates two problems:

Human digestive acids do not break down flesh properly, because they are not strong enough to do so. Therefore, most of the nutrients available in meat are not even absorbed into our bodies.

The undigested remains of meat are sent through our intestines where they can be absorbed into our bodies, but because the intestinal tract is so long in humans, the meat starts to rot before it can reach that stage. What we end up absorbing are the poisons in the rotten meat.

If you must eat meat, chew it thoroughly, as the enzymes in your saliva are very important in the digestive and absorption process. Saliva is believed to release Prana from foods, allowing it to be absorbed through the mucus membrane in the mouth.

Canned foods should be avoided. By the time the food has gone through processing and refining, it has lost 82% of its proteins, amino acids, and nutrients.

Frozen food, especially meat, is even worse. Between stock fed tetracycline, steroids, processing, and freezing, there is a 92% loss. Most importantly, you cannot freeze or can Prana. Frozen and canned foods *appear* fresh because of the chemicals added to preserve the food. T.V. dinners, junk foods, and fast foods should be avoided. All chemical preservatives should be considered poisons.

Sugar, salt, and white flour are worthless. There is no food value left in these after refining, only the chemicals used in the process. Monosodium glutamate (MSG) damages the nervous system and destroys brain cells.

Rely upon vitamin tablets only when the proper vitamins and/or minerals cannot be extracted from food. Most vitamin tablets are chemicals, and the body has a hard time dealing with unnatural substances. They should not be taken in place of food; they are not living energy. Remember what's been said about Prana.

Multi-vitamin supplements are useless, because certain minerals and vitamins prevent the absorption of others, which may be included in the same pill. Take your vitamins separately, at different times of the day, and make sure that they are not synthetic forms of vitamins. Synthetic vitamin D is particularly troublesome to some people. The best policy is to eat the right foods – preferably raw materials.

This chapter addresses things that most people believe have nothing to do with magick or the Great Work, but I assure you they are mistaken. The furnace the alchemists referred to is the body! Ensuring that it functions well is of great importance.

If you take the time to care for your vehicle, you will see a body that is leaner, stronger, healthier, and more resistant to the stressors of a harmful environment and everyday life. Such a body is better equipped to deal with whatever you encounter on your magical voyage, a body worthy of the Great Work.

FASTING

For many centuries, those seeking communion with God have fasted, and magicians often used fasting as a form of self-sacrifice to guarantee a successful magical result. In these times, fasting has become a method to rid the body of toxins.

Water fasts are extremely dangerous to your body. Depending on your physical or psychological condition, water fasts are known to produce hallucinations, delusions, spiritual experiences, euphoria, and other symptoms associated with psychosis. If you are to refrain from consuming foods, then juices and teas are an excellent source of nourishment while the body is being purged of poisons. Fasting is not for everyone; you should consult a physician before radically modifying your diet.

In Biblical times, fasting was widely used to induce these psychotic states. Men have been described in holy books as going into the desert without food or water, and coming back more enlightened or internally changed by some mystical experience. It is the opinion of scholars that the lack of nourishment is what brought about these altered states of consciousness.

Other cultures, such as some Native American tribes, achieved the same experiences using various natural drugs (such as mushrooms or peyote), or herbal mixtures containing hallucinogens. This is probably much safer than a water fast lasting more than ten days.

There are many safe methods and techniques for successful fasts that will not cause physical damage. The following method can be kept up for months, and is relatively safe.

This method is easy as well as safe, and you can keep it up for weeks at a time. Eat only every other day. On the fasting days, drink as much water, juice, or tea as you wish, but remember that most juices contain high concentrations of acid, which could cause heartburn and other gastric disturbances.

The digestive enzymes in your stomach will be diluted relative to how much food you consume. For this reason, on the days that you eat, refrain from eating meats or other fatty foods, because these are not as easily digested and will remain in your body for longer periods of time. Obviously, spicy foods should be limited to avoid acid indigestion.

Exercise

"It is only by labor that thought can be made healthy, and only by thought the labor can be made happy; and the two cannot be separated with impunity."

— John Ruskin

Physical exercise helps to maintain the chemical and organic balance between the body and the mind. When these two are out of synch, disease occurs. For too long, the body and mind have been erroneously treated as two separate units, completely independent of one another.

The brain maintains perfect body temperature, synchronizes the heartbeat with the pulmonary rhythms, and performs many other miraculous functions without us being conscious of it. The brain executes these functions using two components simultaneously. The nervous system executes certain tasks with the use of electricity, and the lymphatic system accomplishes the same objective by using chemicals produced by the glands. Either way, things get done.

If you are physically able, seriously consider martial arts as a form of exercise. This accomplishes two goals. Because it involves the whole body, you will exercise muscles you did not even know you had. Also, there is a spiritual side to the martial arts, and if you have a good instructor, you will learn the virtue and honor of a true warrior.

If, for some reason, you decide that martial arts are too intense or your body isn't capable of dealing with it, try yoga. This will address the same objective, treating the brain as a muscle that, if not used, will wither away, just like physical muscles. There are many types of yoga. Find the method(s) right for you, but remember, those that require physical activity are best.

Yoga: The Magick of the East

Though reading and conversation may furnish us with many ideas of man and things, yet it is our own meditation must from our judgement.

— Dr. I. Watts

Magick is the yoga of the West. The goal is the same, but the methods are slightly different.

The main groups of yoga are:
    Hatha Yoga – Health yoga, bringing the nerves to a calm state
    Raja Yoga – Mental Yoga, concentrative
    Nana Yoga – Yoga of Knowledge
    Karma Yoga – Yoga of work (karma comes from the Sanskrit word
        kri, which means 'to do')
    Bhakti Yoga – Yoga of devotion, to see God in all things
    Mantra Yoga – Yoga of speech
    Dhyani Yoga – Yoga of meditation
    Kundalini Yoga – Yoga of the life force
    Tantra Yoga – Sexual Yoga

The object of yoga is to stop all mental processes, including itself. Yoga is the art of unity and love. When object and subject are united, knowledge occurs.

The process of yoga is as follows:
    Dharana – fixing the mind on an object
    Dhyana – uniting object and subject
    Samadhi – the result of uniting object and subject; union with God
    Samyama – the result and accomplishment of all of the above

There are eight ways in which the magician can achieve Samyama:
    Yama – Control, restraint
    Niyama – Restraint of the mind
(The object of these two is to stop all emotion or passion from disturbing the mind)
    Asana – Posture; "that which is firm and pleasant"; any posture
        which is "steady and easy"

Pranayama – Control of breath; a process whereby all impurities are thrown out of the body

Pratya Hara – General examination of thoughts which one wishes to control

Dharana – Fixing the mind on a single point whereby the impurities of the mind are thrown out

Dhyana – uniting the object with the subject

Samadhi – The result of uniting object with subject; union with God

It seems that all hermetic art and science, whether we are talking about magick or yoga has recently suffered from the spiritual poverty we face in our present day. The very few people that DO speak of it with high regards are usually charlatans or groups of charlatans (cults) looking to gratify their own need for external validation in the form of devotees or members, on the one hand. On the other, it is offered as just another form of exercise that can be purchased online or on TV in the form of DVD's, or get-rich-quick scams.

Like magick, yoga is a science and an art. Like magick, it has a real world use. Like magick, it is a discipline that leads its adherents toward the goal of discovering who we are, our place is in the grand scheme of things and how to unite with our highest self so that we may reach our highest potential. Like magick, it is not a religion. It is a means to an end; a living tradition that belongs to no one and everyone. It addresses the most common disease of our time: the sadness, fear and insecurity created by accepting our potential according to the limitations of our bodies and minds. Yoga can free us from those limitations.

If there is one thing you remember about what I have said about yoga, I hope it will be that man is a spiritual creature. And that the more he tries to convince himself of the contrary the more he commits himself, his fellows, and the human race to a backwards trajectory toward some of the ugliest times we struggled so hard to transcend. One doesn't need to be a prophet to see that we stand on a crossroads. Some would say a brink. Both magick and yoga, when applied with sincerity and the desire to be "more than human" can pave the way toward a much brighter future for the human race. And after all we have been through, all of the suffering, carnage and often unspeakable acts of cruelty against others, don't we deserve the right of moving toward our idealized selves?

The Senses

We do not see things the way they are but as we are.
— Jewish proverb

Most people possess five senses: sight, touch, smell, hearing, and taste. These can be attributed to the five elements; hence, they also find their place in the points of the pentagram.

There is a sixth sense believed to reside within us all. There is indication that this sense is transmitted in the genes, because some strongly psychic people have had strongly psychic children. It is conceivable that this sense is made up of all the information sent to the brain by our other senses. They gather together in our subconscious mind to create a separate, independent sense, which furnishes any missing data relative to any experience.

When human beings were in the early stages of evolution (before the use of language), we possessed a powerful form of telepathy. It was the only way that we could communicate with one another. As the use of language became more prominent, telepathy diminished and we slowly ceased to use it.

The use of the senses is an evolutionary process designed to help the species deal with problems. Most parts of the brain that science is familiar are dedicated to processing electrical signals sent by our senses.

If the unused percentage of the brain can be used as a scale by which to measure human evolution, it becomes clear that as a species, we've got a long way to go.

There are ways to exercise this forgotten sixth sense and regain its use. The method that I have successfully used proved to be a wonderful way to do this. I call it "isolation." It is a form of sensory deprivation.

The method is simple. Isolate all senses but one, by preventing stimuli from reaching the other senses. and focusing your attention on the particular sense you have chosen. A blind man may develop acute hearing and sensitive touch, while a deaf man often possesses incredible senses of sight and smell. This is because the consciousness (energy) required to operate the lost sense has been diverted to the healthy ones.

Imagine how much we could heighten the senses by alternately depriving each of them! Deprivation of the five will surely make you aware of the sixth.

This is not a new method. Egyptian adepts subjected their students to a similar method, making them spend days inside pyramids. There would be no light, no sound, no odors or tastes. This proved to be a dreadful experience to all but a few well balanced individuals. Let me explain something, which must be clear. When the brain is denied stimuli from the senses, it will improvise with data that has been stored in the subconscious. Visions, voices, flavors, and odors are not unusual when performing these experiments. It is even possible to feel things on your skin. It would be foolish to attempt this work without having first become adept with the Lesser Banishing Pentagram Ritual and having prepared your mind and body with Pranayama.

The single most important objective of this exercise is to enhance the senses so much that you can take them with you on the astral plane, where you must exercise complete control over your astral body. Exploring the astral is a beautiful experience when you can see it. It is much more enjoyable when you touch it, hear it, smell it, and taste it.

It's been theorized that the astral and etheric bodies are made up of ectoplasm; only in rare cases can others physically see this. The more of yourself that you bring into the astral, the denser, stronger, and more visible the astral body will be.

Another word of warning: if at any time you hear, see, feel, or otherwise experience something unpleasant, you must make it stop. The most effective way is the Star Ruby. Remember, these impressions must be willed and must not be allowed to manifest until the magician calls them into consciousness. Keep in mind that any image whatsoever is a projection of your own subconscious mind. It cannot exist any other way! These impressions, when properly understood, can lead to better knowledge of yourself, and this must always be your goal.

There are many things at your disposal that you can use to isolate your senses: earplugs, blindfolds, nose plugs, etc.

Because our skin is so sensitive to pressure, temperature, and pain, I recommend the use of a floatation tank. Asana works moderately well, but it is uncomfortable and often painful unless you have mastered it. There are places you can rent time in a floatation tank for a nominal fee.

On the flip side, there are just as many things to enhance your senses: music, the sound of the wind blowing on the trees, or the sound of the birds at sunrise. The taste of fruit and the fragrances of nature. The texture of bark, earth, and rocks, or the softness and temperature of the air as it caresses your body. The coolness of the water and the heat of the sun.

When working with sight, start with a living thing, such as a tree. Look at it; I mean *really* look at it. Notice the different shades of green and brown. Try to see its aura. Is it more visible on the trunk or on the leaves? Find the true beauty in all things that you encounter; they are there for your pleasure. Also, keep in mind that no two people ever see the same object in exactly the same light. You will soon realize how much we normally don't see and how much we take for granted! Do similar exercises with the other senses, always depriving the senses you wish to de-emphasize. Keep records in your diary. After some time, you will have trained your mind to fix its energy on one sense while depriving the others without the use of the tools mentioned above, and this will help you even on the physical plane.

We begin programming our senses at birth, when we have little experience in the physical plane; as a result, our limited knowledge feeds us false information. That is why the sages of ancient times always insisted that all is an illusion.

To illustrate this point, try this experiment:

1. Take a glass of *hot* water and place it in front of you on your left side.
2. Take a glass of *cold* water and place it in front of you on your right side.
3. Take a glass of *room temperature* water and place it in front of you between the other two glasses.
4. Put the forefinger of your left hand in the hot water and keep it there (naturally, you will feel heat).
5. Put the forefinger of your right hand in the cold water and keep it there (naturally, you will feel cold).
6. Take both of your fingers out of the hot and cold glasses and put them both into the glass containing the water at room temperature.

The finger that was once cold will now feel hot, while the finger that was hot will now feel cold, even though the water they are now in is neither cold nor hot. This experience is an illusion.

This is why we have to reprogram our senses, using the knowledge we have today. The exercise above will help to accomplish this.

There is yet another illusion that we face on a daily basis: *the illusion of color.* When we look at a tree, we see the color green in its foliage because that is the color reflected by the leaves. This means that all other colors except green have been absorbed. In reality, you are not seeing the tree, but a reflection of the tree. Everything we see is Light. We perceive light in the same manner that radar perceives sound, except that instead of picking up noise bounced off objects, we pick up light reflected from them. The true color of the leaves on the tree must then be every other color except green (which is not absorbed, but reflected).

By working with color wheels and using a little imagination, we see the true essence of things. We have overcome the illusion. We see things for what they are. Alchemists call this process "The First Matter."

Meditation

Without going outside, you may know the world. Without looking through the window, you may see the ways of heaven. The farther you go, the less you know. Thus the sage knows without traveling; He sees without looking; He works without doing.

– Tao Te Ching

Webster's New Collegiate Dictionary defines "meditation" as:
- To focus one's thoughts on: reflect on or ponder over
- To plan or project in the mind: to engage in contemplation or reflection.

Miguel de Molinos, the Catholic priest mentioned earlier who lived in Italy in the 17th century, wrote that there were two kinds of prayer: outward prayer, which meant you physically pray with your voice, and inward prayer, which Molinos preferred over the other.

This inward prayer involved sitting in a quiet space and contemplating God. This writing angered Church officials, because Molinos' preaching could be interpreted to mean that confession to a priest was not necessary if one confessed to God Himself using inward prayer. As a result, Miguel became popular with the people of that era. He became something of a hero, because his teachings attempted to liberate the people from the Church, which tried to oppress them and used confession as a tool for blackmail.

The Church jailed Miguel de Molinos for life. His book was banned, and anyone caught reading his book was excommunicated, all because he wrote that inward prayer was more efficient than outward prayer. The inward prayer Molinos spoke about was meditation.

To meditate, all you have to do is contemplate an object and hold it in conscious focus for as long as desired. Your mind will start to recall data having anything to do with the object being contemplated, and by careful analysis of this data you can get deeper meanings of the object. Stress is reduced, and it creates nerves of steel, as well as increases concentration. So you see, it's not as hard as most people think. Or is it?

It is perfectly normal for the mind to rebel when you try to restrain it. If this does not happen at first, you are not doing it right! When this occurs, allow the mind to run amuck for as long as it wants to. Eventually, (after about six or seven 15-minute sessions), you will start to notice that the random symbols the mind used at first to overwhelm you have slowed down. Persevere until you can focus your attention on the chosen object for at least 15 minutes without interruption; then, you are almost there.

It is extremely valuable if the first object you start with is one you have a lot of interest in. It will make it easier for you to maintain focus on it. See the chapter on Practical Exercises.

Magical Formulae

The spirit is the master, imagination the tool, and the body the plastic material.

— Paracelsus

The basic principles for Magical Ritual are as follows:

- *Intent* - Decide what you want to accomplish.
- *Classification* - Find the sephirah to best encompass the intent.
- *Research* - Look up the attributions to the sephirah in *Liber 777 and Other Qabalistic Writings of Aleister Crowley* (Samuel Weiser, 1986).
- *Preparation* - Set up your temple, incense, oils, and weapons. Bathe, and don your robe.
- *Banish* - Perform the Lesser Banishing Ritual of the Pentagram and the Lesser Banishing Ritual of the Hexagram.
- *Conjure* - Conjure the proper God using the Greater Hexagram Ritual.
- *Transformation* - Assume that God form. Embody all of the characteristic properties of that God. Become it.
- *Invoke* - Invoke the archangelic and planetary influences connected with the sephirah.
- *Command* - Command the Archangelic and planetary forces to bring the desired effect and demand its completion. (This must be done only when you are certain that the transformation has occurred successfully.)
- *Banish and End* - Banish using the Lesser Banishing Pentagram and Hexagram Rituals. Avoid lust of result; assure yourself of the success of the operation and forget about it.

Ritual Timing

"Time is the chrysalis of eternity."

– Richter

For the most part, practicing magicians place little emphasis on timing, with the exception of the phases of the Sun and Moon. However, there is folly in ignoring the rhythm of time. Research confirms that cycles do occur throughout the day. For example:

Until 1960, when Caesarian births became the preferred method of delivery, 65% of all births occurred between 4:00 and 6:00 AM.

Surveys have shown that the awareness level in most people peaks at noon, when the Sun is at its zenith. Awareness plays such an important part in ceremonial magick that the practitioner should become conscious of which times of day enable his best performance. This is one of the functions of the diary.

Aside from performing rituals when the appropriate planet is visible, there *are* no rules regarding timing. However, in magick, you must surround yourself with every possible element that your subconscious will recognize as a correspondence of the planet you are working with. Therefore, by attributing timing to planetary elements, you add another symbol to your arsenal. I work within the following guidelines:

Because of the strong magnetic field around the Earth, it is best to wait until at least 24 hours after the New Moon before doing invocations. Anytime before or after this is okay. However, the *best* times for invocations are when the Moon is reflecting the most sunlight.

It is best to do your rituals on the days that correspond to the planet (see table, page 162). Planetary rituals should be performed when the concerned planet is either in conjunction with the Sun or when the planet is on the horizon. In general, be conscious of where the planets are at any given time.

Pick a day for rest. Fast if possible on that day. Burn incense to your Holy Guardian Angel, light a candle in its honor, or perform some other form of devotion. "Inflame thyself in prayer."

The Psyche

The mind is a mysterious form of matter secreted by the brain. Its chief activity consists in the endeavor to ascertain its own nature, the futility of the attempt being due to the fact that it has nothing but itself to know itself with.

– Ambrose Bierce

The psyche is made up of three different parts of consciousness, which reside within the brain. In most people, these parts work independently unless they are forced to work together as a result of psychological trauma. They have highly specialized functions and once they are understood, they can be taught to work together to create a more complete and efficient individual. The three parts are:

The *Conscious Mind* is symbolized as The Magician Tarot card. It is the rational mind, which in most of us operates normally during our waking hours. It is the reasoning mind. It is the state in which we *enter* our meditations. It draws edited information from the subconscious in an effort to make rational decisions based on past experiences. If there is ever any discrepancy between the subconscious and the conscious mind, the subconscious always wins.

The *Subconscious Mind* is symbolized by The High Priestess Tarot card. The function of the subconscious is primarily to act as a defense mechanism. It functions at all times, without rest, but it is most prominent while we sleep. It stores all information and experience, but does not allow unlimited use of its data by the *conscious* mind. It works without any effort on our part. It will take any suggestion, sort out all of the possibilities, and draw conclusions based on those suggestions, even if the suggestion is false.

It is important to remember that the subconscious cannot be ordered; an indirect route is required. The subconscious is better reached by way of symbols. Some words are not allowed to enter into the subconscious realm. If words are used in a suggestion, one must never use negative words such as: *no, not,* and *never.* If you give yourself a suggestion, such as "I will not smoke," the subconscious will remove the word 'not' before it stores the suggestion, and it will store the words "I will smoke." It does not parse the negative.

Suggestions must be given without lust of result, or the subconscious will interpret the suggestion as an order and will rebel against you. The subconscious is the place we *pass through* in our meditations.

The *Superconscious* is symbolized by The Fool Tarot card. It is the higher unconscious, the source of *all* consciousness. This is where the Higher Self is supposed to reside, the home of deity within, the palace of the Holy Guardian Angel. This is the House of God, the place we *seek* in our meditations.

The brain should be considered a receiver capable of tuning in to the proper thought wave. It can be conditioned to tune to higher forms of thought waves. The conditioning of the brain is the *goal* of our meditations.

The home of the sixth sense is the right side of the brain. It is speculated that the right brain digests incoming stimuli and compares it against already stored information.

These impulses are stored like the information on videotape, using images and symbols rather than text. The comparative process is instantaneous, estimated to occur within about one-tenth of a second.

The left side of the brain consults with right, and the result of a match is a feeling that you've been here before, or "I know this guy," or "I know how this works." Recognition.

This function of the brain has the power to generate a complete thought form, even though it is blurred by inadequate data. If there is no reference regarding an object or situation, the brain improvises (see section on "Courage"). Because it is a highly visual process, it is strongly linked with our emotional triggers, hence the gut feeling.

This function's main purpose is to create order from chaos. It puts experiences and information in their proper places, then executes a series of experiments to predict an outcome.

This is why those who have strong awareness of this function are most likely to develop an accurate method to utilize this situation to its fullest. The magician sharpens this mechanism through yoga, meditation, sensory deprivation, and similar disciplines.

The sixth sense can command with authority, even though it can at times be wrong. Do not let what seems to be a failure in this function lead you to drop it or disregard it. It could save your life.

From the beginning of our lives, we have been trained to disregard this sixth sense. In fact, as children, many of us were punished for following our instincts. Over time, man has all but evolved out of this primal function.

If you sense something about a person you don't like, listen to your intuition. This should not automatically close your mind to getting to know the person; in fact, the subconscious will insist on overwhelming evidence that there is nothing wrong with him.

As you study the magical arts, your right brain will be fed a tremendous number of symbols, pictures, and principles. It will sort them out, put them into sequence, and store them as video-like images to be recalled when the need arises. Symbols are ingenious keys by which we can access stored crucial information.

We have learned to shrug off this primal instinct of survival, yet it is a crucial part of all geomancy. We must now learn to bring back what society has forced us to disregard as delusion and psychosis.

Here is a simple formula we can use to communicate with the psyche to attain a desired result. It should be used in conjunction with the magical formulae (page 152):

- *Intent* – Decide the purpose of the meditation and suggestion.
- *Classification* – Find the sephirah to best encompass your desire.
- *Preparation* – Use everything at your disposal related to the sephirah to inundate your senses with the essence of your desire. For example, use things like incense, fruits, and music.
- *Presentation* – Delineate a symbol using the appropriate color and any other information best suited to convey your desire to the subconscious mind. (See *Practical Sigil Magic* by Frater U. D., Llewellyn Publications, 1990. This is an excellent source of information on how to design and charge sigils.)
- *Pranayama* – In a relaxed state, situate your body in any position that is rigid but comfortable. Begin controlled breathing.
- *Visualization* – Bring to mind the symbol you have designed and hold it there in your consciousness. *Do not allow your mind to wander.* Remember that the subconscious mind is watching. Hold this mental image for as long as it is comfortable.
- *Affirmation* – Assure yourself that every picture you bring to your subconscious will be manifested.
- *Forget About It!* Your subconscious must be allowed to take the ball and run with it. Any apprehension, skepticism, or anticipation will be decoded as lust of result and interfere with the process. Let the High Priestess handle it from here on. Do not allow the lust of result enter into the picture. This procedure can be used in conjunction with the technique laid out in the section on "Magical Formulae."

The Robe, the Altar, the Diary, and the Holy Oil

All ceremonies are, in themselves, very silly things; but yet a man of the world should know them. They are the outworks of manners and decency, which would be too often broken in upon, if it were not for that defense, which keeps the enemy at a proper distance. It is for this reason that I always treat Fools and coxcombs with great ceremony: True good breeding not being a sufficient barrier against them.

– Chesterfield

Much nonsense has been written about how and where to acquire the materials for magical implements. You could get discouraged if you tried to follow the instructions in medieval literature. The rationale behind making this task so difficult is based on the premise that the more work you put into these tools, the more detail the subconscious mind will absorb with regard to the object. These objects are animated, by virtue of focus and contemplation, to a level that transforms them into an extension of the magician, living things. To match the level of this integration, those who purchase their implements will have to spend several months, maybe even years, meditating on their tools.

This process of tool creation need not be a tedious one; it is enough that you refrain from purchasing a ready-made tool. Don't worry if you do not feel capable of undertaking this seemingly tedious task. Given enough time, magick will stimulate and free the creative child within.

Remember that these implements are physical representations of your spiritual life. You should treat them with respect. Once they have been consecrated to the Great Work, they should not be handled by any other person. They are not toys; treat them with reverence and they will be of great service. If you feel inclined to show them off to your friends, read the chapter on 'Silence.' The four elemental weapons (Wand, Cup, Dagger, and Pentacle) embody four part of the psyche depicted by the elements: Fire, Water, Air, and Earth (or if you prefer, Yod-Heh-Vav-Hah: Tetragrammaton). They also allude to the four planes of existence: Atziluth (the archetypal plane), Briah (the creative plane), Yetzirah (the formative plane), and Assiah (the material plane).

THE WAND

The Wand is the material depiction of the creative principles of the magician. In short, it is a symbol or token of his Will. To illustrate certitude and unshakable determination, it should be as an arrow. It governs the element of Fire and expresses the abstract process inherent in the plane of Atziluth.

There are many styles and variations of the Wand, especially in Golden Dawn temples where every officer has a Wand or Scepter to illustrate a specific idea or principle. But we will only concern ourselves with the personal weapons of the solo magician.

Since the Wand can be compared in many ways to the phallus, many magicians go to great lengths to make their Wands in the same proportions as the physical organ it represents. The Wand is a symbol for the Hebrew letter Yod (׳), the Father, or Chokmah (Knowledge). Since copper is the metal attributed to Venus, or Netzach (Victory) on the Tree of Life, most fashion the Wand from this alloy in order to allude to the prolific aspects of the Work: "Love is the law, love under will."

For the implement to be useful it must be comfortable, and it should not demand attention that would otherwise be focused on the ritual. For a wooden Wand, I have found eight inches to be a comfortable length, with a width between ¾ and 1 inch. For a solid copper Wand, a diameter of ½ inch is sufficient. After it is consecrated, keep it in a red silk bag.

THE CUP

The Cup is the physical object that portrays the element of water. As the Wand represents the magician's Will, the Cup personifies his Understanding. It illustrates the methodology of the plane of Briah.

The symbol of the Cup represents a female idea; hence, it is associated with the yoni (archetypal vagina). The Cup is a symbol of the Hebrew letter Heh (ה), the Mother. Since it represents Understanding, or Binah on the Tree of Life, it is only appropriate that the diameter be three inches. Silver is the rightful alloy for this instrument, which signals to the Moon, or Yesod (Foundation) on the Tree of Life. It should be deep enough to hold wine without it easily spilling as one moves about.

The message behind the Cup, illustrated by Yesod and Binah, is that the Understanding of the magician is as deep as the waters we call our subconscious; it has deeper significance than day-to-day understanding. After it is consecrated, store it in a blue silk bag.

THE DAGGER

The Dagger is an animation of the element of Air. It is symbolized on the Tree of Life by Tiphareth (Beauty), and its planet is the Sun. The Dagger is a symbol for the Hebrew letter Vav (ו), the Son. It explains the process of Yetzirah (the formative plane), and symbolizes the intellectual capacity of the magician (the reason).

Most practitioners of the Art treat the Dagger as a Martian implement, which dictates judicial authority over demons. This is a job best fulfilled by the Sword, a more advanced implement that will not be discussed in this treatise. The Dagger is uniquely Air; unlike the Sword, it threatens malignant spirits with intelligence rather than force.

The blade should be double-edged, with a length of about eight inches to embody the intellectual properties of the Mercurial sephirah – Hod, Science.

Since human beings have a tendency to accept only principles that endorse what they believe to be reasonable, make the hilt from the Venusian alloy, copper, to balance the illusion of intellectual superiority. The correspondences of copper are best embodied by the sephirah Netzach, Art. It is a gentle reminder that magick is both the science *and* art of causing change to occur in conformity with Will. After the Dagger is dedicated to the Work, keep it in a yellow silk bag.

THE PENTACLE

Like the Cup, the Pentacle also corresponds to the Hebrew letter Heh (ה). It is a symbol of Earth, and it represents the body of the magician, the house of God. It is the magician's sustenance. It exhibits the traits of the plane of Assiah. It is the Daughter.

The Pentacle should be made of beeswax, with a diameter of 8 inches and a thickness of ½ inch. Upon the surface, the magician should carve an image that describes the *whole* of the universe. Nothing should be left out. The whole idea here is to reduce all of those things which the magician perceives as the universe to a minuscule dot. The design need not be as elaborate as Dr. John Dee's – symbols that allude to similar ideas can be combined to reduce the amount of detail. But it is important that it be complete. When you are finished, you will know.

This process may take much meditation, so you should take your time with this implement to avoid having to do this twice. The Pentacle will reflect the magician's subconscious perception of the universe. Once it has been blessed, safeguard it in green silk.

THE ROBE

The Robe is the armor of the magician. It should be loose fitting and comfortable, and it should be of a material that is light, soft, and capable of breathing. Cotton is a good material; so is a poly/cotton blend. However, wool is the best because of its ability to direct astral energy.

The color is a matter of personal choice. One should try to match the color as closely as possible to the sephirah being worked with. This would, however, require that the magician keep ten different Robes, one for each sephirah. For this reason, most magicians use black Robes.

Black is the accumulation of all colors and is therefore appropriate for any working. It is so neutral that it is not likely to distract you in the middle of your Work. Furthermore, black absorbs color; it attracts light by behaving like a solar panel, and it should be used for any ritual designed to fortify the aura, such as the Pentagram Ritual, Middle Pillar, etc.

White, on the other hand, is the absence of all color. It repels light, which makes a great shield, and it should be used when working with hostile forces. I have one of each.

The choice of hood (or lack thereof) is also a personal preference. I favor a hooded Robe because it allows me to feel completely shielded, but some would argue that a hood is distracting because it shifts about on your head.

Whatever details you decide are best for you, remember that the garment should be loose and comfortable. You should never wear any underclothes while wearing your Robe. Wide sleeves look great, but they are in danger of catching fire should you lean over your Altar candles. A zipper may be practical, but you will feel it rub against your skin. The fewer distractions, the better the Robe.

THE ALTAR

The Altar is composed of a double cube. The bottom cube represents the underlying force of the Great Work – Love. The top cube represents the Will of the magician. "Love is the law, love under will," or "As above, so below," and "Kether is in Malkuth, and Malkuth in Kether, but after another manner."

There need not be a division between the cubes. In fact, if it is made as a single, seamless rectangular unit, you can use it to store your implements.

The Altar should be 36 inches (91.44 cm) high, 18 inches (45.72 cm) wide, and 18 inches (45.72 cm) deep. It should be black on the outside to illustrate the *accumulation* of all colors, and white on the inside to depict the *absence* of all color. Plywood or particleboard is perfect. The thickness of the wood should be considered; a heavy Altar will need hidden wheels under it to make it easier to move around. A lighter Altar will not support much weight.

Once the Altar is finished, it can be painted. I have seen one covered in veneer, black on the outside and white on the inside. This move proved to be worth the extra effort, as the surface is virtually stain-proof, it tolerates the heat generated by the incense burner, and wax from candles peels right off.

One side of the Altar should be a door with hidden hinges and a lock. The inside should have a shelf for *The Book of the Law*, incense, charcoal, burner, Pentacle, Cup, candles, and holders. There should be places to hang the Wand and Dagger.

THE HOLY OIL

The anointing oil of the magician should metaphorically represent the desire of the Holy Guardian Angel to join with its lower counterpart, the magician. The magician, temple, and weapons should each be consecrated and anointed with this oil. With this in mind, one should take care to only use the highest quality oils available.

During the Aeon of the Sacrificial Gods, the oil used to embody the current of the times was Jerusalem Oil. This was composed of equal portions of frankincense and myrrh, both traditionally used in burial ceremonies.

The fragrance mentioned above is dated, and the New Aeon magician should resort to an essence that best depicts the joy and strength of the Age of the Child. The following is a formula for such an oil. It is named after its creator, the 17th-century magician, Abramelin.

In a glass vessel, mix four parts cinnamon oil, two parts myrrh oil, one part galangal oil, and seven parts olive oil.

If fine oils are used in the proper proportions, the mixture should have a clear, golden appearance. It should tingle slightly. If it stings, it can be diluted by adding more olive oil, but you should only resort to this if it causes serious discomfort. Now for a word of warning: *cinnamon oil is very caustic.* If you keep your oil in a plastic bottle, it may melt and ruin your Altar or some other thing that you have devoted a great deal of time to. Use only glass receptacles.

THE DIARY

The magical Diary should only contain data pertinent to magick – that is, everything. Every entry should start with the date, time, year, and solar and lunar positioning. It should contain all of your feelings, what you ate that day, the weather, etc. These things may not sound important now, but if you are trying to duplicate an experiment it will be necessary to recreate all of the elements that may have played a role in the original operation.

For this reason, take care to choose words that convey your message as clearly as possible. Writing in code may add to the romance and mystery associated with magick, but if your Diary does not convey enough information to reproduce experiments, then all is lost.

Since the days of the week are representations of the seven ancient planets, it is handy to write the planetary symbol associated with the day of the week instead. For example:

THE PLANETARY DAYS & SYMBOLS

Day	Planet	Symbol
Sunday	Sun	☉
Monday	Luna	☽
Tuesday	Mars	♂
Wednesday	Mercury	☿
Thursday	Jupiter	♃
Friday	Venus	♀
Saturday	Saturn	♄

The following is an example of a thoroughly composed diary entry.

♀ *April 8th, 1994 ev.* ☉ *in* ♈, ☾ *in* ♓

3:59 am. Could not sleep. Read email, and sat down for Four Fold Breath (FFB), Aum Madni Padmi Hum Aum (AMPHA) and meditation on feather. Better. Held image for about 4.5 minutes. Mind still wanders, usually to job preoccupation.

4:20 am. This time, 5 minutes or so. Mind still wanders, but it is taking longer to do so. Decided to let mind wander after meditation as "reward." This seems to work, in terms of allowing me some concentrated time, since it expects to be allowed to roam without restriction. Curious that the mind begins to associate all images connected to the feather... automatically analyzing everything using Qabalistic correspondences.

6:15 am. RESH at patio facing the trees and stream as the sun rose over the hill. Beautiful.

6:25 am. Off to catch bus.

11:00 am. Walked casually for 28 minutes. FFB + AMPHA. Still sweating profusely, which is odd, because I am not walking that hard. It has to be related to FFB. Breathing is not as labored as in the beginning, but still lightheaded slightly. Began to zone out after what seemed to be 15 or twenty minutes. The whole process was automatic.

11:45 am. Lunch. Vegetable burger. Walked for 30 minutes while FFB and AMPHA. Lunch ruined by coworker who can't seem to do his job. Will probably have to stay later than usual today to clean up his mess.

1:00 pm. RESH in empty office. Tea.

8:15 pm. Home sweet home. Dinner was waiting for me. Grilled cheese sandwich and soup.

9:00 pm. Read Holy Books of Thelema. Liber Tzaddi. One of my favorites.

9:30 pm. Bed.

Practical Exercises

EXERCISE IN MEDITATION

Let's suppose you have chosen an apple, as I did many years ago, as
your first subject/object of focus.

1. Sit in a comfortable asana and start by relaxing your body, quiet-
   ing your thoughts and regulating your breathing. You have to be
   able to relax in order to meditate.
2. When you have stilled your mind and body, try to visualize a
   shiny bright red apple against a black background.
3. Focus on it and bring it closer so that you can pay attention to
   the detail on its skin.
4. Try to smell it.
5. Try to feel it.
6. Try to bite it and taste it.

In short, try to experience the object fully. Unite with it. All of this
takes place in your mind. The next step, once the inner senses have
had their fun with the object, is to allow your mind to recall data related to the object. Study and analyze each bit of data, but keep your
third eye always focused on the object. If you allow your vision to drift
to another theme while you are analyzing data, your mind will recall
symbols connected with the new theme and you will mix the symbols.

Lotus Asana

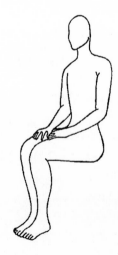

God Asana

Do not allow this to happen! Purity of thought means not allowing the mind to drift from one symbol to another unless the symbols are somehow connected. The union of object with object comes much later in your magical training. The first step is the union of subject and object.

It is easy to become discouraged during this phase of training, but I must convey how important this Work is. A few tips to make things easier for you:

Do not meditate lying down. If you become bored, you will fall asleep. If you do this a lot, it will become a conditioned reflex so that every time you attempt to meditate, you will sleep instead.

In the beginning, fix your attention on only those things that interest you. It is easier to occupy the mind with things it finds pleasant. I find the Tarot to be so full of esoteric symbolism that it is the best training aid I can recommend. I suggest the deck illustrated by Frieda Harris under the instruction of Aleister Crowley (*The Thoth Deck*). The colors are superb and the pictures have a positive effect on the psyche. Later, when you have sufficient control over your thoughts, move on to harder objects.

Whenever possible, begin your meditations after midnight. The world sleeps, and the psychic interference that is present when others are worrying about making it to work on time, making money, paying bills, and keeping their wits about them in the mundane world won't be there to disrupt your Work.

Some people recommend the use of a mantra. If you intend to use one, make sure that your mantra does not become so ingrained into consciousness that it becomes the object of all your meditations. Sometimes these habits are hard to break. The mantra AUM is the most popular. The object of the mantra is twofold. For most people, it is an audible form of focus. What they often don't realize is that it also stimulates certain parts of the brain by vibrating the bones in the head. People who have used mantra swear by it; I personally believe that it silences the internal dialogue.

The Lesser Ritual of the Pentagram (page 171) is specifically made to create a Work area. You may want to do one of these before meditating and one again after meditating.

In the beginning, try to feel about meditation the way you felt as a child when opening gifts on your birthday. Once you have overcome the obvious obstacles to meditation, you will be enthusiastic enough not to need any other reason to meditate other than the pleasant feeling associated with it.

Don't give up until you are successful. It does not take as long as you may think to become proficient at this. I have seen people showing all the obvious signs of success, just to watch them give up the practice *right before they achieve their goal!* If they only knew how close they were, they would have never given up.

Remember, in magick we subject our minds, bodies, and nervous systems to extraordinary energy levels. Meditation prepares us for the journey by disciplining our minds. The ability to meditate is probably one of the most important parts of our Work. It may one day allow you to communicate and look into the eyes of your God.

The Astral Temple

Build a castle in a tranquil place in your mind. It should be made from square stone, and surrounded by water. Equip it with a drawbridge that opens and closes at will. The chain for the mechanism of the drawbridge, you must forge yourself, in your mind. Know every link in that chain.

The dwelling should have a master's quarters, a stable for your fine stallions, a servants' room, a meeting place where you and your knights can discuss battle plans, a furnace for forging, a kitchen (also made from rock), and rooms for your knights' squires and guests.

Brick by brick, stone by stone, you must build this castle, taking time to remember each brick as it was cut and laid down, its texture, weight, etc. Smell the mortar; remember its consistency. This will take effort at first, for it requires a great deal of concentration and planning. You must remember everything, so that when you withdraw from this meditation you are able to return to it and pick up where you left off.

You will tire after a while, but I assure you that if you continue this meditation to its completion, you will find that it was not a mere exercise in concentration.

There is no time limit; it could take a lifetime to finish this Work alone. The important thing is not to leave the Work until it is completed.

When you have finished this abode, you must assign a King to it, as noble, powerful, and wise as you could ever hope to be if you were King of this kingdom yourself. He must be a compassionate man. He will be ruler, judge, priest, warrior, and magician.

Dress him in fine silks, gold, and rubies. Give him power over the castle and the land wherein he dwells. He must be a great leader, an adept in weaponry and master of all he does. Forge for him a beautiful sword, and equally beautiful armor.

Create for him a beautiful woman, with eyes as green as the calm seas. She will be his Queen. Dress her also in fine silks, gold, and rubies. She must possess the same inner qualities as her husband King.

Fill the castle with brave warriors, skilled in their art, and give them chain mail and armor forged by the blacksmiths of the kingdom.

Design a crest of gold, silver, and diamonds, all in a background of lapis lazuli. The crest must symbolically express your inner nature, your love for freedom, your loyalty to your brethren, and your aspiration to your God. Next, make banners and mantles from this crest and give it to your army, so that they shall wear it above their armor in reverence to their King and Queen. Place this crest in the temple, in the King's chamber, in the meeting places for his knights, and in the eating places.

You must be a fair King; see to it that you are kind to your servants, and give your people whatever they need so that they shall want not, just as Lord the Sun provides for all who revolve around Him.

Build your Kingdom on a solid foundation comprised of intelligence, devotion, balance, strength, mercy, understanding, and wisdom. You must possess all these things within before you can put on the golden white crown which will one day make you King.

Astral Travel

As stated earlier, meditation is merely the ability to remember and re-experience specific details communicated by our senses.

Astral travel, on the other hand, is the talent to journey *inward*, and using the abilities mentioned above, to create a space and circumstance whereby the mental body can experience a separate reality, independently of the physical body.

During this transfer of consciousness, the mental (astral) body must be allowed to collect data sent through the senses. In other words, once the separation has taken place, the astral body must be able to see, feel, hear, smell, and taste the new world it is exploring. The following exercises will help to get you started:

Choose a quiet evening and a familiar room where you are unlikely to be interrupted. Remember that you must be passively active, so don't try it when you are tired or you might fall asleep.

Look around you and take a mental photograph of your surroundings. Lay on your back and take a deep breath to help you relax. Loosen all of your muscles, especially your neck. Close your eyes and recall the mental photograph to consciousness. This may take some time, but do not progress until you can focus on this image for several minutes. If you have difficulty, you must spend more time practicing the meditation steps listed above.

Once you have formed and stabilized this image (with your physical eyes closed), focus your attention at the space directly in front of your feet with your mind's eye.

The conscious mind is the paint, the subconscious is the canvas, and the artist is the Self. Imagine a cloaked figure standing at your feet wearing a black, hooded robe. Hold the image as long as you can. It is normal to see it fade in and out, but persist until it remains as solid as the rest of the images around you. Focus your attention on the hood.

Once you have completed *all* of these steps, shift your perspective (consciousness) to the robed figure. Your mind will fight you at first, and glimpses from within the hood will flicker back and forth from both bodies; you may receive sensory input from two places. This is normal, so do not feel discouraged.

After some practice, you will be able to transfer consciousness quickly to the robed figure. When you do, you will be able to see your body lying before you. Don't panic, or you will bounce right back into your body. People have reported being able to see 360 degrees once they have occupied the astral robe.

Once you can remain inside the astral body for long periods, walk around. Touch the walls until you can feel their texture. Pass your hand over the candles, feel the warmth. Smell the incense. Bring all of your senses into play in this practice.

Walk in front of a mirror and pull back the hood. You should see yourself. Don't be alarmed if you don't look exactly as you do with your physical eyes. Remember that sight is an illusion.

After a few minutes, locate your physical body (its right there lying on its back, remember?) and turn your back to it. Lie down on top of it until both bodies have blended together.

Open your eyes, take a deep breath, and banish. Some people like to eat afterward. This practice sounds much more difficult than it really is. It can start out slowly, but once you start getting results it is very gratifying. Don't let failures discourage you from trying again another time. Log both the failures and the triumphs into your diary; your subconscious may be trying to communicate something to you.

The Lesser Banishing Ritual of the Pentagram

I have already explained how the brain tunes in to a specific frequency. The Lesser Banishing Ritual of the Pentagram is a way to get the brain to change frequency. It does this by simply removing your attention from whatever you may be experiencing at that particular time, allowing you to focus your mind on other things. Thus, the original thought or experience has been banished.

This ritual is more an invoking than a banishing, as you will realize when you start visualizing the Archangels. Since the elements are attributed to the senses, there is an intimacy that exists between the Archangels and the parts of the psyche ruling them; thus, during this part of the ritual, the senses are being called to attention. This ritual provides three functions: to create a Work space, to heighten your senses, and to stimulate the brain and kundalini through the use of Pranayama.

To illustrate the importance of this rite, Aleister Crowley once wrote: "Cleanliness is next to Godliness, and had better come first."

To facilitate things, we will break the ritual up into four parts: the Qabalistic Cross, the Pentagrams, the Invocation of the Kerubic Forces, and the Closing.

PART ONE: THE QABALISTIC CROSS

In this segment of the ceremony, you become the nucleus of your own universe by magically establishing pole and equator, and then positioning your heart chakra at their intersection.

1. Face East. With the Sign of Benediction, touch your forehead and say **ATEH** (Hebrew form of 'thou,' attributed to Kether).

2. Touch your breast and say **AIWASS** (the herald of the New Aeon, attributed to Tiphareth on the Tree of Life. When your Holy Guardian Angel reveals Its name to you, substitute that name for Aiwass).

3. Touch your genital area and say **MALKUTH** (Hebrew word meaning 'kingdom,' attributed to Malkuth on the Tree of Life).

4. Touch your right shoulder and say **VE-GEBURAH** (Hebrew for 'and the power,' attributed to Geburah on the Tree of Life).

5. Touch your left shoulder and say **VE-GEDULAH** (Hebrew for 'and the glory,' attributed to Chesed on the Tree of Life).

6. Cross your arms on your breast, left over right, composing the Sign of the Blazing Star, and say **LE-OLAHM, AMEN** (Hebrew for 'To

the ages, Amen').

(The Hebrew in this part of the ritual is the last part of the Lord's Prayer. The crossing of your arms over the breast symbolizes the Rose on the Cross.)

Part Two: The Pentagrams

The proper weapon for this rite is the Air Dagger, not the Sword. The Sword is a symbol of strength and force, useful for manipulating more advanced entities such as demons. The Air Dagger, symbolic of the intellect of the magician, displays intellectual mastery over them.

Pranayama is introduced at this point of the ceremony to increase the amount of oxygen in the blood. When tracing the pentagrams, breathe in deeply with every upward line, exhale with every downward line, and hold your breath for the horizontal line.

Banishing Earth Pentagram

1. Advance to the East, placing your right heel in the hollow of your left foot. Construct the Pentagram of Earth with the proper weapon. (While constructing the Pentagram, remember to inhale deeply through your nose for the upward strokes and exhale slowly through your nose for the downward strokes. Retain the breath for the cross strokes). Visualize the Pentagram as if it were blazing with radiant flames of Fire.

 2. Advance your left foot 12 inches and throw your body forward. Let your hands (drawn back to the sides of your head) shoot out, so that you are standing in the Sign of the Enterer (see illustration). At the same time, stab the center of the Pentagram with the Dagger and vibrate **YOD-HEH-VAV-HEH** (Hebrew for 'Jehovah') with forcible exaltation. Come back to an upright position in the Sign of Silence.

3. With the Dagger still uplifted, turn to the South and proceed as before, but vibrate **ADONI** (Hebrew for 'Lord').

4. With the Dagger still uplifted, turn to the West and proceed as before, but vibrate **EHEIEH** (Hebrew for 'I AM').

5. With the Dagger still uplifted, proceed to the North and vibrate **ATEH GIBOR LE-OLAHM ADONI** (Hebrew for 'To Thee be the Power unto the Ages, O Lord').

6. With the Dagger still uplifted, return to the East.

PART THREE: THE INVOCATION OF THE KERUBIC POWERS

It is probably evident by now that imagination is a key player in this event. Practice visualization until you can clearly see the images and Archangels. Also, to build your astral senses it is important that you use them as much as possible in conjunction with your astral sight.

1. Stand in the Sign of Extended Light. Visualize an Archangel before you, wearing a yellow robe. Remember and re-create the physical feelings associated with a warm summer breeze caressing your body, and say **BEFORE ME RAPHAEL.** The breeze should come from the East.

2. Visualize an archangel behind you, wearing a violet robe. Remember and re-create the physical feelings associated with the ocean spray, coming from behind you, and say **BEHIND ME GABRIEL.**

3. Visualize an archangel at your right side, wearing a red robe. Remember and re-create the physical feelings associated with the heat of a fireplace warming the right side of your body, and say **ON MY RIGHT HAND MICHAEL.**

4. Visualize an archangel at your left side, wearing a black robe. Remember and re-create the physical feelings associated with the taste of an apple, and say **ON MY LEFT HAND URIEL.**

5. Still in the Sign of Extended Light, say **FOR ABOUT ME FLAME THE PENTAGRAMS, AND IN THE COLUMN SHINES THE SIX-RAYED STAR.**

PART FOUR: THE CLOSING

1. Repeat the Qabalistic Cross.
2. Press your forefinger against your bottom lip.
3. Remove your finger from your lips and say **ABRAHADABRA.**

LATIN VARIATION OF THE PENTAGRAM RITUAL

Since the Qabalistic Cross is actually the last part of the Lord's Prayer, which was commonly recited in Latin in Medieval Europe, I decided to include it here to give the reader a variation of the ritual rarely put into practice. The practitioner will notice that in Latin the whole rite feels completely different, with a different purpose than its Hebrew counterpart. Try them both (on separate occasions) and record your findings, feelings, projections, thoughts, weather, etc., in your diary.

PART ONE: THE QABALISTIC CROSS

1. Face East, and with the Sign of Benediction, touch your forehead and say **QUIA TUMM**.

2. Touch your heart and say **AIWASS**.

3. Touch your genital area and say **EST REGNUM**.

4. Touch your right shoulder and say **ET POTESTA**.

5. Touch your left shoulder and say **ET GLORIA**.

6. Cross your arms over the breast, left over right, composing the sign of the Blazing Star and say **IN SECULA AMEN**.

PART TWO: THE PENTAGRAMS

1. Advance to the East, placing your right heel in the hollow of your left foot, and construct the Pentagram of Earth with the proper weapon. (While constructing the Pentagram, inhale deeply through your nose for the upward strokes and exhale slowly through your nose for the downward strokes. Retain the breath for the cross stroke). Visualize the Pentagram as if it were blazing with radiant flames of Fire.

2. Advance your left foot 12 inches and throw your body forward. Let your hands (drawn back to the sides of the head) shoot out, so that you are standing in the Sign of the Enterer. At the same time, stab the center of the Pentagram with the Dagger and vibrate **DEO** (Latin for 'God') with forcible exhalation. Come back to an upright position in the Sign of Silence.

3. With Dagger still uplifted, turn to the South and proceed as before, but vibrate **DOMINUS** (Latin for 'Lord').

4. With the Dagger still uplifted, turn to the West and proceed as before, but vibrate **SUM** (Latin for 'I AM').

5. With the Dagger still uplifted, turn towards North and vibrate **QUIA TUMM EST REGNUM ET POTESTA ET GLORIA, IN SECU-LA. AMEN.** (Latin for 'To Thee be the Power unto the Ages, O Lord').
6. With the Dagger still uplifted, return to the East.

PART THREE: THE INVOCATION OF THE KERUBIC POWERS
1. Visualize an Archangel before you, wearing a yellow robe. Imagine a summer breeze caressing your body as you say **PRO MEO RAPHAEL.**
2. Visualize an Archangel behind you, wearing a violet robe. Feel the mist of the ocean spray as you say **PONE MEO GABRIEL.**
3. Visualize an archangel at your right side, wearing a red robe. See the eternal fires that blaze about in the hearts of men and say **AD DEXTRO MEO MICHAEL.**
4. Visualize an archangel at your left side, wearing a black robe. Taste the fruits of the fertile Earth as you say **AD SINISTRO MEO URIEL.**
5. In silence use your inner voice and say **QUOD CIRCUM MEUM PENTAGRAMA FLAMARE, ET COLUMNA STELLA SEXTUPLUS STARE LUCERE.**

PART FOUR: THE CLOSING
1. Repeat the Qabalistic Cross.
2. Press your forefinger against your bottom lip.
3. Remove your finger from your lips and say ABRAHADABRA.

The Sign of Osiris Slain
(Sign of Extended Light)

The Sign of Isis Mourning

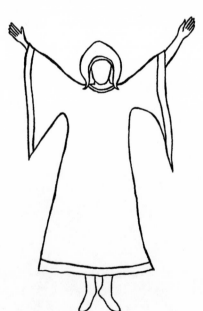

The Sign of Typhon

The Sign of Osiris Risen

THE LESSER BANISHING HEXAGRAM RITUAL

1. Stand facing East with your Wand at your breast and say:
I.R.N.I.
YOD, NUN, RESH, YOD.
VIRGO, ISIS, HOLY MOTHER.
SCORPIO, APOPHIS, HOLY FATHER.
SOL, OSIRIS, SLAIN AND RISEN.
ISIS, APOPHIS, OSIRIS: IAO.
2. Still facing East, form the Sign of the Extended Light and say
THE SIGN OF OSIRIS SLAIN.
3. Form the Sign of the Swastika and say **THE SIGN OF THE MOURNING OF ISIS.**
4. Form the Sign of Isa the Adorant and say **THE SIGN OF APOPHIS AND TYPHON.**
5. Form the Sign of the Blazing Star and say **THE SIGN OF OSIRIS RISEN.**
6. Form the sign in step 2, and then follow it with the sign in step 3 as you say **L.V.X, LUX, THE LIGHT OF THE CROSS.**
7. Advance to the East and trace the Unicursal Hexagram (below) with your Wand, draw in a breath, throw your hands and body forward into the Sign of the Enterer and say **ABRAHADABRA**. Imagine the Hexagram shooting forth and a five-petaled rose blooming in its center.
8. Repeat the same steps to the South, West, and North.
9. Facing East, repeat steps 1 through 6 again.

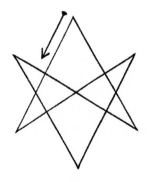

LIBER XXV: THE STAR RUBY

This is absolutely a martial ritual, with emphasis on the number five (Geburah). Unlike the Lesser Banishing Ritual of the Pentagram, the Archangels are of Chaldean origin. Use this ritual to get rid of unwanted things. You should eventually substituted this rite for the Lesser Banishing Ritual of the Pentagram, as it is more effective and goes far beyond the elemental realm.

This ritual is written in Greek. I have attempted to write it phonetically to simplify things for those unfamiliar with the Greek language. However, I strongly recommend learning the alphabet and its correspondences, as a great many Western holy books have been written in Greek.

THE CROSS

1. Face East and inhale deeply. Press your right forefinger against your bottom lip.

2. Sweep your hand out and away from you, expelling your breath forcibly with the cry **APO PANTOS KAKODAYAMANOS**! (Flee from me all evil spirits!)

3. Touch your forehead and say **SOY** ('Thou', same as Ateh).

4. Touch your groin and say **O PHALLAE** (Phallus, Father, Man, Human, Creative Energy).

5. Touch your right shoulder and say **ISJUROS** (Strength, same as Geburah).

6. Touch your left shoulder and say **UJARISTOS** (Thanksgiving, same as Chesed, etc.).

7. Clasp your hands in front of you, interlocking your fingers, and cry **IAO** (Greek equivalent of **IHVH**).

THE PENTAGRAMS

1. Advance to the East and imagine a Pentagram flaming on your forehead. Perform the Sign of the Enterer and, as your hands pass by your eyes, fling forth the Pentagram and roar **THERION**.

2. Do the same thing in the North, but say **NUIT**.

3. Do the same thing in the West, but hiss **BABALON**.

4. Do the same thing in the South, but bellow **HADIT**.

5. Returning to the East, perform the signs of N.O.X. (Vir, Puella, Mulier, Puer, Mater Triumphans), and sing **IO PAN**.

POSTING THE GUARDS

1. Extend your arms in the Sign of Extended Light and say lowly but clearly:

PRO MU YUNGUS ('Before me Jungus').

OPPISO MU TELETARCHIE   ('Opposite me Teletarchie').

EPIDEXIA SINOKIS ('At my best hand Sinokis').

EPIRRISTORA DIAMANOS ('At my other hand Diamanos').

FLENGAE GAR PERI MU HO ASTERTON PENTE ('Flames all around me the Star of Five').

KAI EN TE STELLE HO ASTERTON HEX ESTEKI ('In the column it stands the Star of the Six').

2. Repeat the cross.

The Sign of Vir
(The Father)

Slightly hunched over, facing forward with the head, both hands are closed with the thumb extended. Hands are placed at the temples with thumbs facing outwards like horns.

Also called: Pater or Amoun. The sign of Pan.

The Sign of Puella
(The Daughter)

The Sign of Mulier
(The Mother)

Standing upright with hands open, place right hand over the breast, and the left hand over the groin.

Also called: Venus Pudica. The Sign of Chastity.

Arms bent slightly to form an ark above head, as if holding a huge disk. Hands open. Feet are spread about shoulder width apart. Head facing upwards.

Also called: The Sign of Babalon.

The Sign of Puer
(The Son)

Standing straight, the right arm forms an "L", hand is closed and thumb points towards the head. Left hand is closed and rests at the pelvis, thumb points away from the body.

Also called: Khem, Horus and Mentu.

The Sign of Mater
Triumphans
(Mother Triumphant)

Head looking down towards left breast. Thumb and index of right hand pinches the left nipple. Left hand as if cradling a baby.

Also called: Isis Rejoicing, Isis with Horus.

Pranayama: Controlling the Breath

THE FOURFOLD BREATH

1. Choose a rigid but comfortable position in which you are not likely to fall asleep.
2. Take in a few deep cleansing breaths, and clear your mind.
3. Place your right thumb against your right nostril so that it closes it off. Don't pinch, push.
4. After exhaling all of the air from your lungs, inhale through your left nostril for a count of four. By the time you reach four, your lungs should be filled to capacity. It may take practice to develop a rhythm; pace yourself.
5. Hold for a count of four.
6. Move your thumb away from your right nostril and push your right forefinger against your left nostril. Exhale through your right nostril for a count of four.
7. Hold for a count of four.
8. Inhale through your right nostril for a count of four.
9. Hold for four counts.
10. Move your forefinger away from your left nostril and push your thumb against your right nostril. Exhale for four counts.
11. Repeat steps 1-10 for about 15 minutes.

After you get used to this exercise, it may become necessary to change the count to six, then eight, etc. I have found the use of a metronome invaluable. Just set it for a rhythm that feels comfortable.

Liber Resh

This is a solar adoration that should be performed four times daily. The Sun has always represented the highest ideal of human consciousness: Godhood. Because the physical Sun is responsible for all life on the planet, it is easy to see why the ancients revered it. Most ancient texts (including the Bible) contain descriptions of God that are undeniably congruent with that of our Sun.

The following adoration is multi-purpose. One is to serve as a constant reminder of the Light without which we would be nothing, and to encourage the practitioner to radiate that same Light to those in need. *See Signs and God-forms on page 186 and following.*

At Sunrise, embrace the Sun in the East in the sign of the Blazing Star – arms crossed over your chest, right over left. In a loud voice, say:

> Hail unto thee who art Ra in thy rising,
> Even unto thee who art Ra in thy strength,
> Who travelest over the heavens in thy bark
> At the uprising of the sun.
> Tahuti standeth in his splendour at the prow, and
> Ra-hoor abideth at the helm.
> Hail unto thee from the abodes of night!

At Noon, welcome the Sun in the South in the sign of Fire. Extend the fingers of both hands, joining your forefingers and thumbs, so that they form a triangle. Place this triangle upon your forehead. In a loud voice, say:

> Hail unto thee who art Ahathoor in thy triumphing,
> Even unto thee who art Ahathoor in thy beauty,
> Who travelest over the heavens in thy bark
> At the mid-course of the sun.
> Tahuti standeth in his splendour at the prow, and
> Ra-hoor abideth at the helm.
> Hail unto thee from the abodes of morning!

At Sunset, greet the Sun in the West in the sign of the God Shu. Hold your arms up to each side at shoulder height, then bend them into right angles at the elbow. Place your hands facing up slightly upward, as if you were supporting something above your head. In a loud voice, say:

> Hail unto thee, who art Tum in thy setting,
> Even unto thee who art Tum in thy joy,
> Who travelest over the heavens in thy bark
> At the down-going of the sun.
> Tahuti standeth in his splendour at the prow, and
> Ra-hoor abideth at the helm.
> Hail unto thee from the abodes of day!

Finally, *at Midnight;* recognize the Sun in the North in the sign of Water. Hold the tips of your thumbs and forefingers touching, making a triangle. Place the triangle on the solar plexus, so that the apex of the triangle is pointing down. In a loud voice, say:

> Hail unto thee who art Khephra in thy hiding,
> Even unto thee who art Khephra in thy silence,
> Who travelest over the heavens in thy bark
> At the mid-night hour of the sun.
> Tahuti standeth in his splendour at the prow, and
> Ra-hoor abideth at the helm.
> Hail unto thee from the abodes of evening!

Every single one of these adorations should be followed with this affirmation:

Unity uttermost showed!
I adore the might of thy breath,
Supreme and terrible God,
Who makest the gods and death
To tremble before Thee:
I, I adore thee!
Appear on the throne of Ra!
Open the ways of the Khu!
Lighten the ways of the Ka!
The ways of the Khabs run through
To stir me or still me!
Aum! Let it fill me!
The light is mine; its rays consume
Me: I have made a secret door
Into the House of Ra and Tum,
Khephra and of Ahathoor.
I am thy Theban, O Mentu,
The Prophet Ankh-af-na-khonsu!
By Bes-na-Maut my breast I beat;
By wise Ta-Nech I weave my spell.
Show thy star-splendour, O Nuit!
Bid me within thine House to dwell,
O winged snake of light, Hadit!
Abide with me, Ra-Hoor-Khuit!

The Sign of the Blazing Star
(East-Dawn)

Egyptian God Ra
(East-Dawn)

The Sign of Fire
(South-Noon)

Egyptian God Ahathoor
(South-Noon)

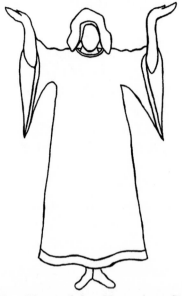

The Sign of the Egyptian God
Shu Supporting the Sky
(West-Sunset)

Egyptian God Tum
(West-Sunset)

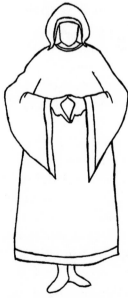

The Sign of Water
(North-Midnight)

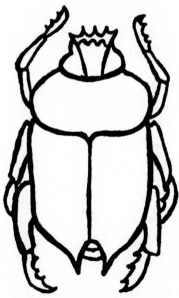

Egyptian God Khephra
(North-Midnight)

Curriculum: Preliminaries

1. After about one month of practicing the Lesser Banishing Ritual of the Pentagram and Pranayama, choose for yourself a Magical Motto. This aspiration-based name may be phrased in Hebrew, Latin, Greek, Enochian, or any other language, including English. Find one that Qabalistically describes your inner nature best.

If, after about a year, you feel that you must change your motto as a result of increased knowledge, do so. But wait at least a year. Record your name in your Magical Diary and use it whenever you perform ritual.

2. Acquire your robe, altar, and elemental weapons. If it is within your talents, you may prefer to make your own implements (see page 157). Magical items made by he who uses them are much more powerful in the hands of the magician. When you manufacture these things, you focus on the details of the tool. All data pertaining to the feel, weight, consistency, and temperature of the implement is fed into your sub-conscious with little effort on your part. This energy is absorbed into the implement, which becomes an extension of your consciousness.

3. Design a ritual to declare your intention to embark on the adventure of self-awareness. Let the forces of the universe know you are dedicating yourself to growth. As with any magical operation, prepare the item to be purified and consecrated (in this case, your physical body) and prepare the temple. See to it that they are both clean.

Bathe your body and banish the temple using the Lesser Banishing Ritual of the Pentagram or the equivalent; burn incense therein. Write your aspiration on a piece of paper and burn it in a silver plate on your altar at the end of the ceremony. Bury the ashes near an oak tree, and say: "This mighty tree will be a symbol of my devotion and dedication to the Great Work. As it weathers the rains, drought, hunger, and time itself, so will I weather the demons that will tempt me to sway from the path I have chosen. To the glory of your ineffable name, AUM." Remember to always start the Work with a banishing.

4. Write a history of your existence, your life story. Write it in the third person, as if you were writing about someone else. It's an effective method to remain objective.

Concentrate your efforts on events that dramatically changed the course of your life, the things that made you the type of person you are now. Leave nothing significant unwritten. The more painful the experience, the stronger the impact it will have had on your life. By analyzing certain events, it may be possible to discover where you are headed. This, in turn, will bring you the knowledge of your True Will.

5. Once you feel finished with your biography, it is an excellent practice to continue as though you were writing a story. Continue until you are finished with the future person's life. Create an adventure using the data and circumstances your life has given you thus far, but always indicate in the manuscript when you started the projection of the future by using a different color ink, for example. This practice will divulge your deeper thoughts concerning your understanding of your True Will.

Write down all aspects of your everyday life. Reveal everything – after all, no one will see it but you. Put a mark next to things you have difficulty perceiving as spiritual. Be honest. Study the reasons behind the lack of godliness in those actions, and work on them using invocation, poetry, mantra, or some other form of devotion until you perceive every act in your daily routine as an act of worship to your God.

If you had a strict Christian upbringing, you might find yourself questioning your sexuality, but remember: in the eyes of the consecrated, everything is holy.

Remember to write everything you did in your diary; if for some reason you want to reproduce the experience, it will be necessary to duplicate all steps of the process. The importance of a diary cannot be overstressed. Magick is a science. Keep notes on your experiments. (See the section "The Diary," page 162.)

6. Memorize correspondences.

7. Write a short study on each of the popular religions. Concentrate on the myth and what it demands from its followers. When you are finished, compare notes and see what they have in common, but most importantly, record how you respond or react to each dogma and why.

8. Learn and practice Liber Resh or an equivalent adoration to the Highest.

9. Practice Pranayama.

10. Practice and gain control over your astral body.

This may seem like a lot of work, and it is. But I assure you, as you accustom yourself to this routine, you will employ 'muscles' in your brain that may have been long forgotten. These exercises will stimulate parts of your brain that, in most people, have lain dormant since childhood. If you are serious about magick, you have everything to gain and nothing to lose from the activities listed above.

Ten Gates to Self Initiation

By now, I hope I have illustrated that Qabalah is much more than a system of correspondences – it is a complex initiatory network.

The disciplines below were first conceived after I had the irritating realization that knowledge alone is not enough to propel the explorer toward The Holy City. Qabalistic principles must be applied consciously, through physical involvement, to assist the psyche in its quickening.

These practices are composed of simple meditations and rituals, and are fashioned to allow you to experience the sephiroth one fruit at a time. The recommended reading will reveal important factors pertaining to the influence of each sephirah on the human experience.

The full implementation of these guidelines will cause subtle but profound and desirable changes in the psyche. You will be initiating yourself.

To avoid overload, you will need to dedicate time to each sephirah. Avoid the temptation to jump around from sphere to sphere abruptly. Give yourself time to fully absorb the subtle energies released by your involvement with them. Take time to smell the roses. When I initiated myself through this process, I allowed 31 days for each sephirah.

Rather than trying to convince you of the value of these practices, I will merely report that, due to their simplicity, I have repeated them often. And each time I have, many priceless jewels have been revealed to me.

The sephiroth are experienced from Kether to Malkuth. This is known as the Lightning Flash. Like all magical work, it is best not to pursue it unless you are committed to finishing it.

1. KETHER *Who am I? Where did I come from? Where am I going?*

Humans are typically created from one sperm and one ovum. Millions of sperm are released during a single ejaculation. A woman will release approximately 400 eggs in her lifetime, usually one during each monthly cycle. Using this information, ponder the following questions: (There *are* no answers; the benefit comes from pondering these points.)

A. How many potential lives do *not* reach conception in a couple's lifetime?

B. What were the odds of the precise egg and sperm that created me coming together?

C. Would 'I' exist today if I had been composed of the same parents but a different egg and spermatozoa? Who would I be? Would I think and behave differently?

D. Meditate on the Infinitely Large and Infinitely Small.

E. Record everything in the Magical Diary.

2. **CHOKMAH** *Develop a mantra.*

A. Use the mediation techniques in the section on meditation until you can still the mind.

B. Just before reaching a state of nothingness, you will hear a noise. Attempt to mimic that sound using your vocal chords. It can then be used as a tool to swiftly enter those states.

C. Attempt to spell the sound you heard, and apply the methods of Gematria to derive a numerical value for the sound.

D. Look up the correspondences in *Liber 777* (Crowley 1986) or *Godwin's Qabalistic Encyclopedia* (Godwin 1994).

E. Record all of your findings and experiences in your magical diary.

3. **BINAH** *Sorrow or Joy?*

A. Meditate on the cycles of birth, life, and death. Compare those thoughts with the scientific hypothesis that energy can only be changed, not destroyed.

B. Contemplate the different stages of feminine development as demonstrated by the archetypal Lover, Wife, Mother, and Crone.

C. Select and perform one of the following:
1. Create a work of art. Take care to put as much of yourself into it as plausible. Take pride in your creation. Allow it to reflect your expertise. Then give it away anonymously.
2. If you have a garden and grow food, take your harvest to a homeless shelter, and give it away anonymously. Only take what you have grown. Buying food for this purpose will not have the same effect.

D. Make an image that appropriately represents the creative feminine powers of Nature. Use natural materials, such as wood, stone, or clay. Place it in the woods, near a steam, or at some other secluded place. Decorate the location by propping wild flowers against the icon. Do not tell anyone where it is. Do not concern yourself with the possibility that it may be found; it will either be torn down or adored by individuals unknown to you, and this is what you want to happen. Visit the location frequently, taking care to brush away fallen leaves and remove other debris from the space. Burn myrrh or civet incense, and offer flowers or fruit to it until it is taken or destroyed by strangers.

E. Record all feeling, findings, and other experiences in your magical diary.

4. CHESED *Practice benevolence.*

A. Perfect the art of forgiveness. To forgive is not to lose, but to gain. Begin by forgiving yourself for what ever afflicts you. True forgiveness, when the offender is sincere, does not humiliate because one does not expect anything in return except the release of malignant energy.

B. Contemplate the aspects of your God.

C. Think about how your God might expect you to behave if you were Its Priest or representative.

D. Study the functions of your body, particularly its power to absorb the nutrients that help create new cells. Compare your findings with your mind's ability to absorb information.

E. Perform *Will* before all meals. (See Appendix.)

F. Write your thoughts and experiences in your magical diary.

5. GEBURAH *Develop self-discipline.*

A. Examine every action you make. Look for habits, and look within to see how you benefit by having them. Don't be critical of other people. You are not working on them – you are working on yourself.

B. Destroy or replace unwanted or destructive habits by exercising your willpower. Do not give in.

C. Only allow thoughts into your consciousness that are conducive to Knowledge and Conversation with the Holy Guardian Angel.

D. Contemplate the virtues of right conduct.

E. Contemplate your body's ability to eliminate waste, and compare your findings with your mind's ability to exclude ideas contrary to its aims.

F. Record everything in your diary.

6. TIPHARETH *Encourage the imagination.*

A. Choose a day when you are likely to be free of domestic and work-related responsibilities, and walk through nature for several hours. The more isolation from other people, the better. Imagine you are a newborn – you have never seen any of the wonderful things unfolding before you. Try to see the world through the eyes of an infant.

B. Seize the opportunity to bring harmony to disputes between friends or family members, so that all involved parties gain equal satisfaction and peace of mind.

C. Continually perform solar adorations, such as *Liber Resh,* to materialize the ability to assume god-forms while identifying yourself as one and indivisible with Our Lord the Sun.

D. Record *all* pertinent information in your magical diary.

7. NETZACH *Make elemental contacts.*

Do not banish; this is not the place for routines. In fact, it should feel more like a celebration. Your first contact can be very enjoyable if you keep it unconstrained by formalities. Remember, Netzach is the sphere of the emotions, Bhakti Yoga, and sympathetic magick. The absence of ceremony in this exercise shouldn't surprise you. Use your creativity. Earth spirits are called Gnomes. Air spirits are known as Sylphs. Water dwellers are dubbed Undines. Fire creatures are called Salamanders.

The following example is for earth. Make the appropriate adjustments for the other elements. For example, Air can be encountered on a high mountain top or the roof of your apartment building on a windy day. Go to a river, creek or the ocean for Water; even your bathtub will work. Fire can be experienced by lighting a camp fire in the hills, or even by sitting in front of your fireplace.

EARTH

A. Go to the mountains (or some place away from people and distractions) and find a cave or a clearing on the ground.

B. Grab a handful of soil and roll it around in your fingers, taking care to notice its consistency and color. Smell it. If you are really zealous, taste it. A little dirt never hurt anyone.

C. Once you have flooded your conscious with this element, allow yourself to become passive but aware, and use your knowledge of the element to improvise a proper conjuration for Earth. Do this with emotional intensity until you feel you have made contact with the spirit.

D. Ask your elemental contact to provide you with a way to contact it in the future. Try to get its name.

E. Thank your contact, and politely give it license to depart.

F. Record your perceptions and experiences in your diary.

8. HOD *Practice Ceremonial Magick.*

A. Learn the mathematical theory of magical symbols.

B. Learn the numerical value of letters, and develop an understanding of Gematria.

C. Devise talismans for each of the Elements.

D. Invoke the elemental contacts encountered during the Netzach working, but this time, use ceremony and talismans. Keep a high level of temple decorum. Be kind.

E. Record you every word and movement in your magical diary.

9. YESOD *Explore the unconscious.*

A. Learn astral projection.

B. Make a scrying device. (See "The Magical Mirror")

C. Develop your own techniques by using the scrying device.

D. Begin recording dreams in your magical diary.

E. Examine and question all impulses.

F. Record developments in your magical diary.

10. MALKUTH *Know and care for your body*

A. Stand naked before a full size mirror. Explore your body thoroughly.

B. Be constantly conscious of everything you put into your body. Omit harmful things from your diet.

C. Start a regimen to improve your physical condition. Begin a fitness program or yogic discipline.

D. Try to find similarities between human bodily functions and the objective of nature (perpetuation).

E. Begin the ongoing task of creating your Life Beads (See *Liber Vitae*).

F. Record *everything* in your magical diary.

Making and Using the Magick Mirror

A Magick Mirror is any object with a surface that lends itself to use as a projection screen for the unconscious mind. Many people use crystal balls, quartz, or glass.

Several years ago, while exploring a forest in southern Oregon, I stumbled across a huge, spherical, black rock about the size of a bowling ball. I was delighted to find that it was solid obsidian. I later found a lapidary who was willing to slice a section out of the center for a nominal fee. The outcome was a one inch thick disk ten inches in diameter. I had one side ground to a slight curve, somewhat like a shallow plate, and then I hand polished it to a mirror-like shine. The result was the best scrying device I had ever owned... or so I thought. It wasn't long before someone broke into my house and stole it.

Push having come to shove, I didn't have time to go rummaging through the forest for another chunk of obsidian; I had to think fast. One must always remember that an object possesses no magical power aside from what the psyche endows it with – no matter how beautiful and useful the item may be.

This is what I came up with, and ended up working better than anything else I had ever used before – including the obsidian mirror.

1. Purchase a large clock face at least 10 inches in diameter. These can be found in crafts supply houses, antique stores, and thrift shops for reasonable prices.
2. Place the glass face down on a piece of newspaper, and spray the back with black gloss paint. Go easy, making sure not to develop runs on the glass. Many small coats is better than one heavy coat.
3. While the paint dries, you will need to build a frame to hold your mirror. The frame will have to be proportional to the glass. I prefer a dark wood (walnut) tripod design, as this elevates the mirror a few inches above the table. To use such a device, sit or stand in a comfortable location and place the mirror near you but away from direct sunlight (which may cause an irritating glare). Fill it about three quarters full with saltwater. One teaspoon of table salt or sea salt works just fine.

For your first few sessions, just stare into the glass and allow your eyes to relax. You can blink as often as you need to; don't tire your eyes. Let your suppressed images form as they will, without fighting. This will allow images needing expression to develop in the mirror, and your psyche will be better off for it. You will know your unconscious has had enough when the images cease to manifest. By necessity, you must then begin training to guide your unconscious to willed subjects. Hold the person, place or thing you would like to know about in the back of your mind and begin gazing. As long as the image you have chosen remains in the back of your mind, you can assume that all images manifesting in your mirror will be somehow connected to the subject.

Once you have gained proficiency at willing the subjects of your images, you can begin using your magick mirror in conjunction with conjuration, allowing you to receive messages from elemental and angelic contacts.

I know many people so adept at these practices that they will see images developing in water bottles while dining at restaurants, or in ponds while visiting nature. This is normal. For our purposes, however, this can present a problem.

The magician must always resist the temptation to allow the mind to manifest images on its own. *All images must be willed, and they must not come unannounced.*

The only exceptions are the times you *consciously* allocate a portion of gazing time for the psyche to wander, to allow it to play. Daily performance of the Lesser Banishing Ritual of The Pentagram will prevent problems from occurring. If you find your vision blurring as you stare out your car window on a rainy day, focus your eyes until the images go away – especially if you are driving!

In the hands of individuals who realize the images are self-produced, the magick mirror is a wonderful, therapeutic tool. In the hands of the superstitious, it can encourage psychosis. The magick mirror will enable a well trained magician to visually appreciate the beautiful contacts and the new friends he has made in the new worlds he has explored.

Liber Vitae

Making a visible object representing the sum of your life to the present, such as a beaded necklace, is a tremendous tool in learning who you are. Over time, it becomes a potent talisman, and because it grows and changes with you and your life experiences, it becomes a physical representation of who you were, are, and are becoming. The unearthed bodies of shamans were often decorated with necklaces believed to be a testament to the shaman's life.

Meditating on individual beads will allow you to re-experience both happy and painful memories, making the necklace a valuable tool for confronting previously ignored issues deeply buried in your subconscious. Gazing at it will occasionally trigger long forgotten memories that continue to negatively affect you in your present life, and you will have the opportunity to work through them.

BIRTH: To begin, chose a bead to represent your birth. For mine, I chose an Egyptian Ankh, which is a symbol for life

LIFE: Next, select an appropriate bead to represent each year of your life. I chose Hematite, because its planetary attribution is Saturn, and it is therefore compatible with Earth. Saturn is the planet assigned to Binah, the Mother of Malkuth. Its element is fire, symbolic of life

INITIATIONS: You will need beads to signify initiatory experiences. I used Malachite for my initiation beads. It is believed that this stone possesses the strength to rearrange human molecular structure. It was also understood to cause changes within an individual by resolving his karma, so it comes as no surprise that the ancients believed the human race would benefit greatly from its use. To me, the benefits of this stone are congruent with the rewards of initiation.

Whatever stones you choose to mark your initiations, they will need to be inserted *following* the beads marking the years that the initiations took place.

I mark only formal initiations on mine; that is, I have marked only initiations performed within the community that best expresses my idea of universal Truth. But this need not always be the case.

A little digression is justified to avoid confusion. *Initiation* means *beginning.* In a spiritual context, initiation is any experience inspiring an individual to rise above normal states of consciousness towards self-knowledge. Initiations are not always pleasant, and don't always appear to contain spiritual jewels, but if the event is, in fact, an initiation, it will always reveal some truth.

We need not be part of an organization or group to receive initiation. The Beloved initiates us through our involvement in life. It uses everyone and everything we encounter as potential instruments for initiation. We are alive to be initiated!

The point is to mark the events that have brought you closer to Knowledge and Conversation with The Holy Guardian Angel. For example:

CHILDREN: If you have ever given birth or fathered a child, mark the event by placing an appropriate bead in the space following the life bead that marks the age you were when you gave life to your child. Whether this is birth or conception depends on your role or personal preference. I chose Lapis Lazuli because of its association with the Egyptian Goddess Nuit, the mother of Horus.

SERVICE: Service beads are used when an individual has dedicated considerable amounts of time to his order, coven, clan, or church. These beads should be placed *in front* of each life bead representing the year the service was rendered. Service is sacrifice, and because of its connection with blood, I have chosen garnet.

DEATH: You should mark the deaths of anyone close to you or whose passing greatly affects you. Unless you are fortunate enough to predict your own passing, you will not place this bead, but you can select which bead is to mark it. While preparing for your adventure, entrust your talisman to a loved one willing to finish the talisman for you. Any emblem of death will do. I have chosen a brass skull.

Appendix 1: Will
TO BE SAID BEFORE ALL MEALS

Head of table: Do what thou wilt shall be the whole of the Law.

Everyone else: What is thy will?
Head of table: To eat and drink.

Everyone else: To what end
Head of table: That I may be fortified thereby.

Everyone else: To what end?
Head of table: That I may fight in the Battle for Freedom in accordance with the Book of the Law.

All: Love is the law, love under will.
Head of table: Fall to.

Appendix 2: Correspondences

Hebrew Letter	English Equivalent	Meaning	Path No.	Letter Value	Tarot Attribution	Astrological, Planetary, or Elemental Correspondence	
א Aleph	A	Ox	11	1	The Fool	Air	△
ב Beth	B	House	12	2	Magician	Mercury	☿
ג Gimel	G	Camel	13	3	Priestess	Luna	☽
ד Daleth	D	Door	14	4	Empress	Venus	♀
ה Heh	H	Window	15	5	The Star	Aquarius	♒
ו Vav	V, W	Nail	16	6	Hierophant	Taurus	♉
ז Zayin	Z	Sword	17	7	The Lovers	Gemini	♊
ח Cheth	Ch	Fence	18	8	Chariot	Cancer	♋
ט Teth	T	Serpent	19	9	Strength	Leo	♌
י Yod	Y	Open Hand	20	10	Hermit	Virgo	♍
כ Kaph	K	Fist	21	20, 500	The Wheel	Jupiter	♃
ל Lamed	L	Ox Goad	22	30	Justice	Libra	♎
מ Mem	M	Water	23	40, 600	Hanged Man	Water	▽
נ Nun	N	Fish	24	50, 700	Death	Scorpio	♏
ס Samech	S	Prop	25	60	Temperance	Sagittarius	♐
ע Ayin	O	Eye	26	70	The Devil	Capricorn	♑
פ Peh	P	Mouth	27	80, 800	The Tower	Mars	♂
צ Tzaddi	Tz	Fishhook	28	90, 900	Emperor	Aries	♈
ק Qoph	Q	Head	29	100	The Moon	Pisces	♓
ר Resh	R	Forehead	30	200	The Sun	Sol	☉
ש Shin	Sh	Tooth	31	300	Judgment	Fire	△
ת Tau	T, Th	A Mark	32	400	The World	Saturn	♄

Astrological Correspondences

Opposites	Zodiacal Triplicities	Planetary Triplicities
♈ ♎	△ = ♈ ♌ ♐	△ = ♂ ☉ ♃
♉ ♏	▽ = ♋ ♏ ♓	▽ = ☽ ♆ ♃
♊ ♐	△ = ♊ ♎ ♒	△ = ☿ ♀ ♅ ♄
♋ ♑	▽ = ♉ ♍ ♑	▽ = ♀ ☿ ♄
♌ ♒		
♍ ♓		

ASTROLOGICAL CORRESPONDENCES, CONTINUED

Exaltations		Planetary Rulership				
♅ is exalted in ♏		Saturn	♄	rules	♑	and ♒
♄ is exalted in ♎		Jupiter	♃	rules	♐	and ♓
♃ is exalted in ♋		Mars	♂	rules	♈	and ♏
♂ is exalted in ♑		Sol	☉	rules	♌	
☉ is exalted in ♈		Venus	♀	rules	♉	and ♎
♀ is exalted in ♓		Mercury	☿	rules	♐	and ♓
☿ is exalted in ♏		Luna	☽	rules	♋	
♆ is exalted in ♌		Uranus	♅	—		
☽ is exalted in ♉		Neptune	♆	—		

Elemental Correspondences

△	Fire	Heat & Dryness	Radiant Enery
▽	Water	Cold & Moisture	Fluids
▵̶	Air	Heat & Moisture	Gases
▿̶	Earth	Cold & Dryness	Solids

Bibliography

Angelo, Thomas A. and Cross, K. Patricia (1993) *Classroom Assessment Techniques: A Handbook for College Teachers*, Jossey-Bass Publications

Bates, Daniel G. and Fratkin, Elliot M ((2002) *Cultural Anthropology* Allyn & Bacon

Bierce, Ambrose (2002) *The Unabridged Devil's Dictionary*, The University of Georgia Press

Chesterton, Gilbert (1959) *Orthodoxy*, Doubleday & Company

Crowley, Aleister (1986) *777 and other Qabalistic Writings of Aleister Crowley*, Weiser Books

Crowley, Aleister (2004) *The Book of the Law | Liber AL vel Legis*, Weiser Books

Crowley, Aleister (1989) *The Holy Books of Thelema*, Weiser Books

Crowley, Aleister (1942) *Liber OZ*, s.n.

Crowley, Aleister (1998) *Magick: Liber Aba : Book 4*, Weiser Books

Crowley, Aleister (1976) *Magick in Theory and Practice*, Dover Publications

Crowley, Aleister (1991) *Magick Without Tears*, New Falcon Publications

Crowley, Aleister *The Libri of Aleister Crowley* http://www.hermetic.com/crowley/ including *The Law of Liberty, Liber Librae*, etc.

Crowley, Aleister; Neuburg, Victor B.; Desti, Mary (1999) *The Vision and the Voice With Commentary and Other Papers: The Collected Diaries of Aleister Crowley, 1909-1914 E.V. (Equinox)*, Weiser Books

Crowley, Aleister, (author), Symonds, John (Editor), Grant, Kenneth (Editor) (1989) *The Confessions of Aleister Crowley: An Autobiography*, Penguin

Fortune, Dion (2000) *The Mystical Qabalah*, Weiser Books

Frater U.D. (1990) *Practical Sigil Magic*, Llewellyn Publications

Graves, Robert (1960), *The Larousse Encyclopedia of Mythology*, Batchworth Press Limited

Jung, Carl *The Psychology of the Child Archetype*

Jung, Carl (1970) *The Structure and Dynamics of the Psyche (Collected Works of C.G. Jung, Volume 8)*, Princeton University Press

Jung, Carl (1985) *Synchronicity*, Routledge

Kaplan, Aryeh (editor) (1997) *The Sepher Yetzirah*, Weiser Books

Lévi, Éliphas (1990) *Dogmes et Rituels de haute magie*, Bussière "Liber Libræ Sub Figura XXX"

Nietzsche, Friedrich (2005) *The Anti-Christ*, Cosimo Classics

Nietzsche, Friedrich (2005) *Beyond Good and Evil*, Digireads.com

Nietzsche, Friedrich (1974) *The Gay Science*, Vintage

Rawls, John (1999) *A Theory of Justice*, Belknap Press

Vivekananda, Swami (1999) *Karma Yoga: the Yoga of Action*, Vedanta Press

Recommended Reading

Alvarado, Louis (1991) *Psychology, Astrology & Western Magic*, Llewellyn Publications

Buber, Martin (1990) *The Way of Man: According to the Teachings of Hasidism*, Citadel Press)

Crowley, Aleister (1986) *777 and other Qabalistic Writings of Aleister Crowley*, Weiser Books

Crowley, Aleister (1998) *Magick: Liber Aba : Book 4*, Weiser Books

Fortune, Dion (2000) *The Mystical Qabalah*, Weiser Books

Godwin, David (2002) *Godwin's Cabalistic Encyclopedia*, Llewellyn Publications

Johnsen, Linda (1994) *Daughters of The Goddess: The Women Saints of India*, Yes International

Kant, Immanuel (1960) *An Immanuel Kant Reader*, Trans. and Ed., with Commentary by Raymond B. Blakney; Harper Books

Kaplan, Aryeh (editor) (1997) *The Sepher Yetzirah*, Weiser Books

Koltuv, Barbara Black, Ph.D (1987) *The Book of Lilith*, Nicolas-Hays Inc.

Lukeman, Alex (1993) *What Your Dreams Can Teach You*, Llewellyn Publications

Moore, Robert and Gillette, Douglas (1991) *King, Warrior, Magician, Lover: Rediscovering the Archetypes of the Mature Masculine*, HarperOne

McLean, Adam (1989) *The Triple Goddess: An Exploration of the Archetypal Feminine*, Phanes Press

Qualls-Corbett, Nancy (1998) *The Sacred Prostitute*, Inner City Books

Regardie, Israel (1995) *A Garden of Pomegranates*, Llewellyn Publications

Soho, Takuan (1986) *The Unfettered Mind*, Kodansha International Scekely, Edmond Bordeaux (1981) *The Teachings of The Essenes from Enoch to The Dead Sea Scrolls*, C.W. Daniel Co.

Scholem, Gershom (1968) *Zohar: The Book of Splendor*, Schoken Books

Ueshiba, Morihei (1992) *The Art of Peace*, Shambhala Publications

Wilson, Robert Anton (1986) *Ishtar Rising*, Falcon Press

Zhuge, Liang and Ji, Liu (2005) *Mastering The Art of War*, Shambhala Publications

Who Is Gerald Del Campo?

Gerald Enrique del Campo (b. 1960) is a poet, musician, songwriter, photographer, magician, philosopher, author, and lecturer on occult and religious topics. He was born in Córdoba, Argentina on January 14, 1960. He immigrated to the United States with his parents when he was eight years old.

Gerald del Campo attended Catholic School in North Hollywood, California when he first arrived to America. During his early school years he showed a special aptitude towards science, mathematics, languages, and religious-philosophical studies. At a very young age, he asked to be prepared for the Catholic Priesthood, but over the years his enthusiasm for Catholicism faded. He began corresponding with the various Rosicrucian Orders, the Martinists, the Center for Self Realization, and an assortment of other groups. During this period he had become acutely aware of an occult movement which was taking place in the 1970's mostly from the warnings of his teachers, and became interested in the subjects of comparative religion, philosophy and metaphysics, all of which led to his fascination with the occult itself.

In 1975, when del Campo was 15 years old, a complete stranger handed him The Book of the Law, which altered his course dramatically. This led him to the direction of Aleister Crowley's writings and Thelema.

From 1982 till 1986, he studied Enochian magic with David Kennedy, Israel Regardie's personal secretary. In 1987 he joined Ordo Templi Orientis, where he eventually became Master of RPSTOVAL Oasis. Later he served that Order in the capacity of Quartermaster and volunteered to serve an eleven year term with the OTO's Electoral College. From 1988 until 1990 he was a member of the College of Thelema and studied under Phyllis Seckler. In 1989, he was a founding member of the Temple of Thelema. In that same year he joined Fraternitas Lux Occulta and studied under Paul Clark. In 1998 he became a member of The Hermetic Order of QBLH. He founded the The Order of Thelemic Knights, a Thelemic charitable organization based on the virtues soldiering and chivalry as exemplified by Templarism on August 23, 1999.

In August 2006, due to conflicts within the Order, Gerald del Campo resigned from the OTO after 20 years membership.

Timeline of Major Events

Joins Ordo Templi Orientis 1987

Becomes a student at the College of Thelema 1988 - 1990

Founding member of Temple of Thelema 1988 - 1989

Master OTO RPSTOVAL Oasis 1989 - 1995

Member Fraternitas LUX Occulta 1988 - 1989

Ordo Templi Orientis Quarter Master 1989 - 1992

Ordained Priest in EGC by Lon DuQuette in Los Angeles on August, 4 1991

New Aeon Magick: Thelema Without Tears is published March 21, 1993

Served as senator in Ordo Templi Orientis Electoral College 1993-2004

New Aeon Magick is adopted by the Pagan Student Alliance at the University of Texas, Austin in 1997.

Member QBLH 1998-2002

QBLH Education Committee 2000 - 2001

Founding Member of Aleister Crowley Foundation 1998

Founder and Grand Master of Order of Thelemic Knights August 23, 1999

New Aeon English Qabalah Revealed is published July 4, 2001

Consecrated Bishop by Ecclesia Gnostic Catholica Hermetica, January 1, 2003

Adopted Tau Apollonius as name January 1, 2003

Founder and Patriarch of the Thelemic Gnostic Church of Alexandria January 1, 2003

Education Committee North American College of Gnostic Bishops June 6, 2003 -2006

Became head of Aleister Crowley Foundation 2004

Ethics committee North American College of Gnostic Bishops March 2, 2006

Resigned from the OTO after 20 years membership August, 2006

Writings

Mr. del Campo is a prolific writer who is concerned with the positive and responsible promulgation of the Law of Thelema. Many of his writings have been translated into various languages and some have become either recommended or required reading at various universities around the world.

Partial Bibliography

The following list include some of his more popular writings in the areas of Thelema, religion, philosophy, and mythology which have appeared in various magical journals are listed in order. They do not include his poetry or dissertations on photography, brewing, or technical writings:

On Animal Sacrifice (1985)

Latin Banishing Ritual of The Pentagram (Winter of 1986)

On the Use of Blood in Ritual (1986)

De Matrimonium et Reconciliato Inter Ingenium et Motus et Fructus Coniunctio Summ (1987)

On The Use of Blood in Ritual (1988)

The Problem With Secular Democratic Politics (July 4th 1992)

New Aeon Magick: Thelema Without Tears (published March 21, 1994 (First edition 1994, Llewellyn Worldwide - Second edition Luxor Press 2000)

Introduction To Qabalah (published on the web in 1996, and becomes recommended reading for a class on Jungian Psychology at the University of Cape Town, South Africa.

Officium De Sacerdotium 1998

Alchemy: The Struggle for Immortality (published on web site in 1998, and it becomes required reading for "Egyptian Chemistry" at the National University of Singapore from 1998-2003

Rabelais: The First Thelemite (1999)

St. Joan of Arc (1999)

Saladin (1999)

Sir William Wallace (1999)

Malcolm X (2000)

Crazy Horse (2000)

Rosaleen Norton (2000)
Mansur al-Hallaj (2000)
Emiliano Zapata 2000)
Hypatia of Alexandria (2000)
The Progression of The Ego Into The Self via The Law of Thelema
    2001)
To Gnow or Not To Gnow (March 2001)
Chivalry Is Not Dead (2001)
Why Thelema Implies Responsibility (2001)
After 9/11 (2002)
On The Importance of Studying The Book of The Law (2002)
To All Children (2002)
New Aeon English Qabalah Revealed (Luxor Press 2001)
Basic Techniques for Performing Sex Magick (2002)
Why Does Religion Get Such a Bad Rap? (2003)
A Short Article of The Subject of Thelemic Gnosticism (2003)
A Brief Introduction to The Religion of Thelema (2003)
Bakhti and The Order (2002 for OTK)
The Sword (December 2002)
A Short Treatise on Buddhism (2002)
A Short Article on The Unfolding of Thelema (2003)
There is No God But Man - Really? (2003)
Soldiers Are Soldiers (2003)
Doing and allowing those to do what one does best (2006)

About Concrescent Press

Concrescent Press is dedicated to publishing advanced magickal practice and Pagan scholarship. It takes advantage of the recent revolution in publishing technology and economics to bring forth works that, previously, might only have been circulated privately. Now, we are growing the future together.

Colophon

This book is made of ITC New Baskerville and Baskerville Old Face using Adobe InDesign, Illustrator and Photoshop. The cover was designed and the body was set by Sam Webster. The illustrations were drawn by the author.

Visit our website at
www.Concrescent.net

CPSIA information can be obtained at www.ICGtesting.com
Printed in the USA
LVOW08s0310080816

499462LV00001B/46/P